AN ALBUM OF The Irish Americans

EUGENE MURPHY AND TIMOTHY DRISCOLL

WILLIAM LOREN KATZ, CONSULTING EDITOR

FRANKLIN WATTS, INC. NEW YORK 1974

An Album Of The Irish Americans

For Our Families

Photographs courtesy of:

EDGAR L. OBMA: 78 (bottom). FABIAN BACHRACH: 72 (bottom). HERBERT BARRETT MANAGEMENT: 60 (middle right). JANUS FILMS: 56 (top right). JILL KREMENTZ: 60 (top right). JUDIE MILLS: title page. LIBRARY OF CONGRESS: 9 (top right, bottom), 19, 26, 28, 32, 37 (top left, middle), 40, 41, 44 (top), 47, 49, 50, 55 (bottom), 68 (top left). MARGARET MURPHY: op. p. 1, 55 (top). MUSEUM OF THE CITY OF NEW YORK: 12 (top), 15, 20 (top—HARRY J. PETERS COLLECTION), 20 (bottom)—J. CLARENCE DAVIES COLLECTION), 23, 31 (bottom), 37 (top right, bottom), 60 (bottom right), 65 (top), 68 (bottom), 80 (bottom —BYRON COLLECTION). NEW YORK PUBLIC LIBRARY: 9 (top left), 12 (bottom), 14, 31 (top), 44 (bottom —THEATER COLLECTION), 56 (bottom right—THEATER COLLECTION). THOMAS MURPHY: 56 (left), 77. WIDE WORLD PHOTOS: 4, 65 (bottom), 71 (top left), 72 (top), 78 (top), 80 (top), 81, 82. UNITED ARTISTS: 60 (bottom left). UNITED PRESS INTERNATIONAL: 75.

Photo Research: Margaret Murphy

Library of Congress Cataloging in Publication Data

Murphy, Eugene.
    An album of the Irish Americans.

    SUMMARY: Discusses the reasons for the Irish migration to the United States, the difficulties faced by these immigrants, and the contributions they made to their new country.
    Bibliography: p.
    1. Irish in the United States—Juvenile literature. [1. Irish in the United States] I. Driscoll, Timothy, joint author. II. Title.
E184.I6M77   917.3'06'9162   73-13994
ISBN 0-531-01519-X

---- ♣ ----

TABLE OF CONTENTS

Introduction
1

THE IMMIGRANT ERA
3

Homecoming
5

The Irish Heritage
6

No Irish Need Apply
11

The Church
17

The Neighborhood and the Saloon
22

The Western Irish
25

The American Civil War
29

The Irish in Politics
34

Organizing the Workingman
38

The Immigrant Bards
42

A Bold Fenian
45

The Fighting Irish
48

THE MODERN ERA
53

Moving Up
54

Latter-Day Bards
58

The Quest — The Irish from Smith to Kennedy
62

Today's Irish
76

Bibliography
84

Index
85

An Album of The Irish Americans

Young and old Irish Americans gather at a "Feis" —
an Irish performing arts festival. Prizes are given at the end of the day
and, as seen in these pictures, the competition is often demanding.

INTRODUCTION

"Fellow immigrants," began President Franklin Delano Roosevelt when he addressed a convention of the Daughters of the American Revolution. These women, we have been told, became angry. It was not then fashionable to be immigrants or ethnic Americans.

Today, Italian Americans, Polish Americans, Black Americans, and others are looking eagerly and proudly for Old Country roots and their place in American history. These Americans hope to find a better definition of who they are through a more precise definition of who their ancestors were.

This book is about the grand old men and women of American ethnicity, the Irish Americans. Because they were among the first immigrants, and were early partners in the building of America, their history will tell much about who we all are today.

We focus on Irish Americans who through their lives and work show much of what it was and is to be both Irish and American at a particular time and place. First we present a collection of men and women, legs planted in two countries, often carrying two flags, exiles from their homeland, and strangers in an adopted land. These are the people of the immigrant era. Then we present the modern Irish Americans, Americans primarily but also conscious of bonds of sentiment and belief that tie them to another land.

Let us first get a few crucial statistics out of the way. How many Irish came to America?

The task of counting the number of Irish in revolutionary America is complicated by the great migration at that time of the Scots-Irish. These people, generally Scottish Protestants who had been installed by the English on confiscated lands in Northern Ireland, were called Irish by the English-born Americans. But these Scots were Protestant, not Catholic like the native Irish, and often regarded themselves as superior to the Irish. The native Irish considered them Scots, and we shall do the same. A fair estimate then of the number of true Irish-born people in revolutionary America is about 40,000.

Official records, which are available beginning from 1820, establish that between then and 1840 about 700,000 Irish-born immigrants entered the United States. Between 1840 and 1860, including the years of the great famine, there were an additional 1.7 million to 2 million immigrants. The fifty years from 1880 to 1930 saw about 1.5 million more. And from 1930 up to 1965, when a new immigration law went into effect, about 6,600 entered each year.

Now, how many Irish Americans are there in the United States today? The 1970 census lists slightly more than 16 million Irish Americans. That is about 8 percent of the total population. Here then is an album of these Irish Americans; some of them great, some of them humble, and some of them rogues.

The Immigrant Era

HOMECOMING

In late June, 1963, John Fitzgerald Kennedy, the thirty-fifth president of the United States, visited Ireland. He was the first Irish-Catholic president and the first American president in office to make that journey. But his visit was far more than an occasion of "firsts" for the millions of Irish and Irish Americans who closely followed the news of that journey. For them and for John Kennedy it was a homecoming.

One hundred fifteen years before, in the midst of a great, crushing famine, President Kennedy's great grandfather had sold all his possessions to buy a one-way boat passage from County Wexford, Ireland, to Boston, Massachusetts, U.S.A. When twenty-five-year-old Patrick Kennedy stepped off the immigrant-crowded packet ship onto the Boston dock, he owned little more than the shirt on his back. But, like all the Irish who came before him and the millions who followed, he had all that poor, starving, oppressed Ireland could give him — an Irish heritage.

Robert Frost, the American poet who spoke at John Kennedy's inauguration, urged the young president to "be more Irish than Harvard." Frost was urging Kennedy to think back beyond his university days, back and back further still to 1848 and that Boston dock full of Irish immigrants. Think of what they had brought to America, Frost was saying.

John Fitzgerald Kennedy, the first Irish-Catholic president of the United States, addresses the freely elected Parliament (the Dail) of Ireland in 1963. Behind him hangs a gift to the people of Ireland — one of the famous green flags carried by the Irish Brigade in the American Civil War.

THE IRISH HERITAGE

We are the music makers,
And we are the dreamers of dreams,
Wandering by lone sea breakers
And sitting by desolate streams;

World losers and world forsakers,
On whom the pale moon gleams:
Yet we are the movers and shakers
Of the world for ever, it seems.

From *Ode*, Arthur O'Shaughnessy
(1844–1881)

Ireland is a small island, most points are hardly more than seventy miles from the sea. About seventy miles off its eastern coast, across the stormy Irish Sea, lies Great Britain. Ireland's other coasts face the seemingly endless and hostile Atlantic Ocean.

The sense of "aloneness" that comes from being an island people is reinforced by the Irish climate and history. During most of the year Ireland is a chilly, wet land. Gray rain clouds regularly fill the sky, hovering low, as if enveloping the land. The summer months, while generally pleasant, are never free of daily rain showers and chilly evenings, and heavy clouds still hang over the nearest hilltop.

The inhospitable seas that regularly have sent storms and freezing winds across the countryside have also brought "strangers," like the Danes, to the island. One man who in A.D. 432 arrived from Rome, came armed only with the Christian religion. He was Saint Patrick. Within a few short years, most of the Irish had turned from their pagan Celtic gods to Christianity. Once converted to the Church of Rome, the Irish were not easily persuaded to worship elsewhere.

In 1169 another kind of stranger came — this time in numbers. The Norman French, fresh from their conquest of England, crossed the Irish Sea and conquered and settled parts of Ireland. Over the next four centuries their heirs in England continued the invasion. Then the Tudor family monarchs, Henry VIII and Elizabeth I, set about in a determined fashion once and for all to subjugate the Irish.

A new reason for the English and Irish to make war had appeared by this time — religion. When the English monarchs broke with the pope in Rome, the Irish had little reason to follow their would-be masters. Instead they held fast to Catholicism. As a result, the English took up the banner of conquest with a missionary zeal.

No Englishman ever crossed to Ireland with greater certainty that God was with him than did Oliver Cromwell. As leader of the anti-royalist forces in England, Cromwell came to Ireland in 1649 to make war on the king's Irish allies. By 1652, Cromwell was victorious and hundreds of thousands of Irish were dead — killed by famine, disease, and Cromwell's soldiers.

Slavery in the West Indies was the sentence for several thousand Irish rebels who survived Cromwell's victory. And for those who remained behind in a conquered land, life without chains was little better.

The conquerors moved quickly to control the land — the real wealth of the agricultural island. Irishmen now paid heavy rents to absent landlords for the privilege of earning a bare living by tending lands they had once owned. Catholics could not buy land, or rent out land if they were fortunate enough to still hold any. None could vote, or work for the government, or serve on a jury, or receive a university education. All, however, were required to contribute to the Protestant Church of England. Catholic schools were outlawed, as were Catholic priests and religious ceremonies. The native tongue of the Irish, Gaelic, was aggressively discouraged.

The oppression was not limited to the political or religious rights of Catholics. Ireland itself became a colony. Its economy was organized to advance the prosperity of the mother country, England. Thus English laws restricted Irish exports that competed with English products and discouraged the development of local industry. Then farmland became the only means of survival, and the peasants became even more dependent on the landlords. Interested primarily in profit, the landlords raised the rents regularly. When new farming methods were introduced, and fewer men were required to tend the land, the surplus hands and their families were mercilessly evicted.

There was nationwide misery. "Never did I behold . . . such dismal marks of hunger and want as appeared in the . . . poor creatures I met on the road," wrote the Protestant bishop of Derry in 1723. Fully a century later, the English novelist Sir Walter Scott saw an unchanged scene. "Their poverty has not been exaggerated; it is an extreme verge of human misery."

What did the Irish do? Some fought back via secret societies like the "Whiteboys" and the "Ribbonmen," striking at night with fire and violence against the landlords. Others, like the Protestant Wolfe Tone, organized Protestants and Catholics alike into the United Irishman to work for, and if necessary fight for, the liberation of their homeland.

When Tone's rebellion came in 1798, it was no more successful than any of the earlier Irish uprisings. Like all of them, it was savagely crushed. Exile was the sentence for many of the rebels who survived. William MacNeven and Thomas Emmet, two leaders of the United Irishman, were exiled to France. From there they made their way to America. Before the nineteenth century closed, over 3.5 million Irishmen would follow these exiles of '98 to a new home in America.

Resistance to oppression in the new century was to take a significantly different form. In 1792, Parliament gave Catholics the vote on the same basis as Protestants, though many other restrictions, both political and religious, remained. This enfranchisement opened the way for the Irish political leader Daniel O'Connell. Working closely

Daniel O'Connell (above left), the liberator of Ireland, led the successful Irish campaign for Catholic emancipation. O'Connell's organizing efforts had provided many Irish immigrants with experience in mass politics that they put to use in America. This picture below of Irish peasants in the 1800s effectively captures the hard, hungry nature of life in Ireland. Farming was difficult on the rough, rocky land but for these people it was the only way to survive. The stone and mud buildings roofed with straw often housed father, mother, children, and grandchildren. Above right, a "Whiteboy" captured by British soldiers, from a nineteenth-century painting. The Whiteboys were bands of Irishmen who terrorized British landlords and others whom they believed were exploiting Irish farmers or peasants. Groups like the Whiteboys, while not organized as revolutionary or political movements, kept alive the Irish spirit of resistance to British rule.

with the church, O'Connell organized the Catholic masses of Ireland into a solid political force able to elect friends of Catholic emancipation. O'Connell himself stood for election from County Clare. Though he won overwhelmingly, as a Catholic he could not take his seat in Parliament. But within a year the British Parliament had passed a Catholic Emancipation Act.

O'Connell, at last a member of Parliament, began a campaign to separate the United Parliament of Britain and Ireland and to restore an independent all-Irish legislature. Earlier Irish patriots had fought and died for this kind of independence. But unlike those who had sought to overthrow the British royal government, O'Connell regularly professed his loyalty to the crown. Just as regularly, however, he criticized royal officials and royal policies. And instead of organizing masses of armed men, O'Connell organized "monster meetings" of hundreds of thousands of orderly Irish men and women. They would listen eagerly as "the Emancipator" preached Irish independence.

This movement for independence never succeeded, however, for nature intervened in a most horrible manner.

The potato was the basic foodstuff of Ireland. It was cheap, easily cultivated in any part of the island, and it fed both man and beast. When the yearly crop failed, as it did in 1821, the entire island suffered. But when a blight destroyed the crop in 1845 and then lingered on for four more years, an incredible famine shrouded the land. Starvation and disease took a staggering toll — at least one million Irish died.

Many of those who survived left Ireland. Some crossed to Great Britain and the European continent. Many made the great journey to Australia and New Zealand. And almost two million came to the United States.

O'Connell had given these immigrant Irish a taste for organized politics, for mass movements designed to change laws and the life of the common man. He had also given them the drive to push and probe in a politically oppressive situation to see how far the opponent would back away.

From Tone and the Whiteboys and so many others, these immigrants had a heritage of striking back violently in an oppressive situation. From the English, the immigrants had learned to believe that the law could be an oppressor and that a shrewd man sometimes winks at the law and does what he thinks best. The immigrants also had learned to trust only each other — to rely first on the family, then on their Catholic neighbors, and after that to be wary.

From each other, the Irish learned to survive, to protect the family and defend the faith, and to hope. In the midst of it all — tyranny, disease, famine — they made music and dreamed dreams.

♣

NO IRISH NEED APPLY

When they arrived in their new land the famine immigrants entered a country that was growing, thriving, bursting at the seams with expansive energy. It was a country that needed them, their willing hands and broad backs, their hunger and their eagerness for a decent life. But it was also a country that was very suspicious and fearful of them because of their great numbers and their religion. Instead of an open door, many Irish, eager for work, found only signs that read, "No Irish Need Apply."

Some Irish had been part of the building of their new land from its earliest days. The Carrolls of Maryland had arrived in 1688. One of their American-born sons, Charles, had signed the Declaration of Independence; another son, John, became the first American-born bishop. John Barry, born in County Wexford, was a Philadelphia merchant captain at the time of the Revolution. The Continental Congress commissioned him the first captain in the American navy. General John Sullivan of George Washington's staff was a grandson of one of the early political exiles. It was Sullivan who countersigned Washington's order designating the March 17, 1776, password — "St. Patrick."

If Irish already had been accepted in America, why the hostility to the newcomers?

The earlier arrivals had come in small numbers and had often been among the most educated people in Ireland. But beginning in the 1820s a steady, increasingly larger stream of Irish immigrants had

been arriving at American docks. These men and women, 700,000 of them by 1840, were poor people driven from their homes by hard times. When the famine years came in the 1840s the stream of immigrants turned into a seeming tidal wave. And the wave carried to America two million immigrants, described by one Irish bishop as "the debris of a nation." These were people who were unskilled, uneducated, poor, and often sick or sickly after the torturous Atlantic crossing. The famine immigrants were in no way equipped to settle easily into the life of the big American cities in which most of them landed.

And neither were the American cities ready for them. Most of the available housing was in cellars and slum buildings. Men and women already sick from hunger and the rigors of a four-to-seven-week sea voyage cramped in airless spaces between decks, became even sicker in damp cellars. If they could work, all that was offered them were the hardest, most dangerous tasks in sewers or construction gangs. Many died because of the conditions under which they worked and lived. (Patrick Kennedy was dead within ten years of landing, leaving a widow and four children.) Others became, as they had been in the Old Country, beggars and paupers. Still others turned to crime. In the 1850s, the Irish, though less than one-third of the total population, accounted for 69 percent of New York City's paupers and 55 percent of its arrests.

As with many immigrant groups that followed them to America, the Irish were looked down upon by early European settlers who considered themselves "native Americans."

Though America provided more religious freedom than did most if not all European countries, many Americans were still suspicious of people with different religions or different traditions. To them the

Above, Irish immigrants arriving in New York in 1855 and debarking from an Atlantic sailing ship. Note the trunk at right labeled "Pat Murphy for Ameriky." This sketch below of an Irish-American slum by a nineteenth-century artist, entitled "Court for King Cholera," graphically depicts the crowded, filthy conditions in which the early immigrants lived. Note the skeletonlike bodies of some of the children, their trashheap playground, and the dead rat they have for a plaything. Note also the stereotyped Irish men in tophats and cutaway coats, with their pipes; and the women in shawls.

Crude buildings like this one above, photographed in late nineteenth-century New York, were often all that was available to house the poor immigrants. In time, some people began to think all Irish lived in shanties, and the Irish themselves began to refer to their poorer cousins as shanty Irish. The Irish, like most other nineteenth-century immigrants, generally crossed the Atlantic in steerage bunks like these at far left. Many died or landed in America too sick to work after a long ocean voyage in such crowded unsanitary conditions. Left, "Tommy": A ragged Irish shoeshine boy photographed by early social worker Jacob Riis in New York City in the 1890s.

Irish were not just poor and troublesome; they were, worse yet, Catholics in a predominantly Protestant land. Prominent Americans publicly questioned whether the immigrants could be loyal to both the pope and the United States. Rallies denouncing the Irish and demanding anti-immigration legislation became weekly events. Some well-known Protestant churchmen regularly preached the dangers posed by the pope-loving Irish.

The secret Know-Nothing party grew from these rallies and meetings. "I know nothing" was a member's required answer to any question about the party. Its anti-Irish and anti-Catholic feeling became for a time a political force. The Know-Nothings were powerful enough to capture control of several city and state governments, Massachusetts among them, and to force the Democratic and Whig parties to pay attention to them.

Not all the "nativists" stopped at preaching and writing. Anti-Catholic riots broke out in a number of cities. Churches and convents were burned.

Leaders within the Catholic Church and the Irish community tried to channel the Irish-Catholic reaction to these threats into constructive educational activities. The immigrants, however, often responded with riots of their own.

The overwhelming majority of Irish immigrants worked, stayed clear of crime, and if they did not prosper, at least they ate regularly. These men built the canals and railroads that were uniting the settled parts of the great American continent. In the cities they built the new streets and the sewerage, lighting, and transit systems. In Pennsylvania, the immigrants became miners; in industrial New England, they worked in the mills. Their wives, widows, and daughters became washerwomen, seamstresses, and domestic servants. (The widowed Brigid Kennedy worked first as a saleswoman and then as a hairdresser to support her family.) The adventurous saved the money they earned on the docks or in construction gangs and headed west to seek gold.

Sadly, despite the backbreaking hard work of the ordinary Irish immigrant, the No Irish Need Apply signs were a long time in coming down.

John Boyle O'Reilly (1844–90), the editor of the *Boston Pilot* and himself an immigrant from County Meath, captured the weariness and despair that marked these early years in America:

I am tired of planning and toiling
In the crowded hives of men;
Heart weary of building and spoiling
And spoiling and building again.
And I long for the dear old river,
Where I dreamed my youth away;
For a dreamer lives forever,
And a toiler dies in a day.

From *The Cry of the Dreamer*

THE CHURCH

In County Wexford, one of the few places where the Rising of '98 succeeded, if only for a few days, the victorious rebel forces were commanded by priests. In the United States, while none was ever seen lifting a pike or leading a cavalry charge, priests were again recognized leaders of the Irish community.

Memories of centuries of oppression directed against them because they were both Irish and Catholic, made the immigrants intensely loyal to their church and to their priests. And the anti-Catholic feeling that met them at the big-city docks only served to reinforce that loyalty.

The priest served the immigrant community in many ways. In addition to being a spiritual guide, he gave financial advice, taught school, and wrote job references as well as letters "home." The immigrant priest, however, was mostly an organizer and a builder. He had to be. Unlike his European counterpart, he inherited neither cathedrals nor universities. He and the immigrants had to build the church in America brick by brick.

The immigrants built not only churches but also the groundwork of America's massive Catholic school system. The public schools of that time were often openly Protestant in their teaching. The Irish, with fresh memories of Protestant schools in Ireland, responded generously when the American bishops decided to establish a Catholic educational system. Elementary schools were followed by high schools and then institutions like Notre Dame in Indiana, Holy Cross and Boston College in the Boston area, and Fordham University in New York City.

Some of the most talented and colorful churchmen in the history of American Catholicism came from this immigrant generation. Tough, outspoken, and Irish-born, John Hughes, archbishop of New York, was a clergyman especially popular among the immigrants. Never one to back down when threatened, Hughes handled the problem of anti-Catholic riots by announcing to the mayor that if a single church were burned, the Irish would take their revenge by setting fire to the city. No Catholic churches were burned.

James Cardinal Gibbons of Baltimore and Archbishop John Ireland of St. Paul, while immigrants like Hughes, were clergymen of a different sort. These two men were in the forefront of the battle within the church and within the Irish-American community to adapt Catholic political and social practices and teaching to American democracy. The Roman Catholic Church was at that time basically a European institution experienced more in dealing with kings and emperors than with freely elected presidents. At a time when some churchmen distrusted democracy and longed for Catholic kings, these two immigrant Irishmen were important progressive voices. "Republic of America," said Ireland, prayerfully addressing the church's Third Plenary Council in 1884, ". . . thou bearest in thy hands the hopes of the human race, thy mission from God is to show nations that men are capable of the highest civil and political liberty."

Gibbons and Ireland also spoke for a group within the early American church, eager to see their fellow Catholics move fully into American life and exert influence in public affairs. In this struggle and others they had the cooperation of such Irish-American priests as Bishop John J. Keane, the first rector of Catholic University, and

Above left, James Cardinal Gibbons of Baltimore: An Irish American who defended the right of workingmen to form unions at a time when other churchmen were calling unions immoral. Above, Archbishop John Hughes of New York, Ireland-born, was a vigorous defender of the rights of his Irish congregation. He once organized an all-Catholic slate of candidates for the state legislature when the major parties failed to provide funds for church schools. The slate lost. Left, Archbishop John Ireland of Minneapolis-St. Paul, once a Civil War chaplain, was a staunch and active Republican. Like his good friend Cardinal Gibbons, Ireland was a strong believer in American democracy and vigorously defended it against the criticisms of churchmen who favored other governmental systems.

Monsignor Denis O'Connell of the American College in Rome. Against them was a coalition of German immigrant clergymen and conservative Irishmen, such as Archbishop Michael Corrigan and Bishop Bernard McQuaid. The German Catholic point of view emphasized maintaining old-country traditions and the German language, and greatly lessened the influence of these German immigrants in the church and in American life.

Gibbons and Ireland practiced what they preached when they had an opportunity to influence public affairs. Bishop Ireland, once a Union Army chaplain, was an active Republican who often campaigned for his party. Upon hearing that Cardinal Gibbons was to deliver a prayer at a Democratic convention, Bishop Ireland warned, "Pray hard for the country, not so much for the party."

Because they were first, the Irish shaped the character of American Catholicism. Later immigrants from Catholic lands, like the Italians and the Poles, would send their children to Catholic schools where they were usually taught by Irish-American nuns and brothers. The priests in their churches were invariably Irish — and often still are. The Irish influence was so great that for many Catholic European immigrants, American Catholicism often seemed a new religion.

The immigrant church was often accused of being narrowminded, defensive, and anti-intellectual. But in reality it was merely practical. There was little time for philosophical and theological speculation. The need was to build a Catholic community and institutions in a strange and often hostile land. The Irish built that early church.

Above, the first American cardinal, 1875. Archbishop John McCloskey of New York receives the symbol of his office — the Beretta that marks the second-highest rank in the Catholic Church — from Archbishop Bayley of Baltimore. The drawing is a Currier and Ives lithograph. Below, St. Patrick's Cathedral, old and new. The first St. Patrick's located in downtown New York City served a Catholic population so small that, as this 1830 sketch indicates, the church could maintain a graveyard on its adjoining land. By 1858, however, the mostly Irish-Catholic population had grown so large that it could build and maintain this magnificent building.

THE NEIGHBORHOOD AND THE SALOON

The immigrants developed two other protective and comforting institutions that, like the church, served them well in the early, troublesome years in America. One was the neighborhood.

Often the immigrant neighborhoods were given names taken directly from the Old Country — names like Kerrytown, an area in Boston, or Cork Hill, in nearby Roxbury. "Cork Row" was an area in New York's Lower East Side. These names emphasized how the immigrants were trying to re-create life as it had been for them in Ireland.

Not all these neighborhoods were so nostalgically named, however. Some of the names, like Hell's Kitchen in New York, said much about the slum conditions in which the immigrants lived.

But within the boundaries of their neighborhoods, the immigrants developed a lifestyle that took a little bit of the pain out of the deprivation they faced every day. If a man died suddenly (as men often did in those hard days), neighbors and relatives would help his family survive. And to mark the death, neighbors and relatives would gather to "wake" the deceased. At an Irish wake, people mourned, prayed, gossiped, and sometimes drank. As Catholics, the Irish were sure that life continued after death, and so their mourning ritual was a comfortable mixture of religion and congeniality, sorrow and hope.

There was also a lively social life. House parties, or "hoolies in the kitchen," were one way of passing a Saturday night. Benefit dances to aid the family of an injured worker or to raise money for a new church were fun as well as financially rewarding. Newly arrived immigrants, "greenhorns," were taken by friends or relatives to these parties or dances to meet potential spouses.

Steve Brodie (with the flat-topped hat), shown here in 1899 in his New York City Irish saloon, claimed to have jumped from the Brooklyn Bridge. Brodie's claim was never proved and it is believed that like all Irishmen, he had a gift for telling tall tales.

The real center of the social life was the neighborhood saloon. Escaping from overcrowded tenements and the long, hard workday, men would meet there with old friends and share immigrant experiences. There, also, they celebrated their survival and advancement in America. The liquor the saloonkeeper served with a willing hand loosened both the Irishman's tongue and his imagination. He talked and he dreamed.

To the great distress of temperance-minded Americans and to the great regret of many Irish families, the Irish had a great, even immoderate, love for the beverage they would call "the creature" or "the jar." One historian discovered that the number of saloons in Boston grew from 850 to 1,200 during the most active years of famine immigration.

Not all the immigrants drank, and most did not drink excessively. But those who did drink did so loudly and boisterously enough to make temperance-minded citizens think that all the immigrants were drunkards.

Often a brawl would result from a happy gathering of the men or, as they might call themselves, the "boyos."

Someone would then call the police wagon and the brawlers would be hauled away. In time, the wagon made so many such trips that it became known as the "paddy wagon" because to the natives all the Irishmen seemed to be called "Paddy." The name still lingers, though the Irish Americans are today much more likely to be driving the police wagon than to be riding in the rear pen.

The saloon also had a political function. It became the urban equivalent of the New England town meeting hall. Every community problem as well as every personal problem was discussed here.

Next to the priest, the saloonkeeper was the most important man in the Irish community. Because of his financial success, more leisure time, and greater social contacts, he often turned his talents and ambitions to politics. Patrick Kennedy's only son, a president's grandfather, was himself a saloonkeeper and ward boss in Boston. One wit said that the easiest way to break up a meeting of a Democratic Party Executive Committee in New York was to scream "Your saloon's on fire!"

THE WESTERN IRISH

Not all the immigrants clustered in the big cities of the East. Some set out from those cities in wagon trains or on the railroad for the farmlands and wide-open spaces of the western frontier. Some others often worked in the cities just long enough to earn the cost of passage before they boarded a ship bound "round the cape" for America's west coast.

Thomas Fitzpatrick was one of the first of the Irish to move out beyond the cities. In fact, he was the guide for the first wagon train to cross the plains to California. Born in County Cavan, Fitzpatrick came to America in 1816 at the age of seventeen. He moved quickly inland to St. Louis and joined a series of pioneering, trapping, and exploring expeditions into unchartered Indian country. One of these expeditions, on which Fitzpatrick was second in command, blazed the trail that later became the primary route to the Pacific United States, the historic Oregon Trail. Later Fitzpatrick served as teacher to another famous trailblazer, Kit Carson. Before he died in a hotel bed in Washington, D.C., this frontiersman served a term as an extremely fair and scrupulous Indian agent.

James Shields was another pioneering immigrant. Born in County Tyrone, Shields arrived in the United States in 1826. Settling first in Illinois, where he studied law and taught, Shields soon became active in the Democratic party. After a term in the legislature, Shields was elected state auditor. After that term, he was elected to the state supreme court. While serving as state auditor, Shields had a dispute with another rising politician, Abraham Lincoln, and challenged him to a duel. Before actually drawing swords, the men discussed the matter, called off the fight, and emerged as friends.

When the United States and Mexico went to war, Shields was commissioned a brigadier general. A "fighting general," Shields personally led his men in many battles and was severely wounded at Cerro Gordo. After a short rest, Shields was back in the smoke of

battle leading an attack on the fortified convent-church of San Mateo. There, the forces Shields commanded succeeded in capturing the "San Patricio Battalion," a unit of American army deserters including some Irishmen enraged by native American anti-Catholicism. The anti-Catholics of course cited the battalion to buttress their belief that the Irish could not be trusted. But the brave performances of Shields and other Irishmen, like Colonel Bennet Riley, Lieutenant John Paul Jones O'Brien, and army guide Thomas Fitzpatrick, belied their rumor-mongering.

After the war Shields returned to Illinois, where a grateful citizenry elected him to the United States Senate. In 1855 he left the Senate and Illinois, journeyed to the Territory of Minnesota, and there founded the towns of Shieldsville, Erin, and Kilkenny. When Minnesota entered the Union one of its first senators was James Shields. And when the Civil War erupted, one of the first men whom Republican President Abraham Lincoln went looking for was his old friend, Democratic Senator Shields. In that war Shields was to command a division in the Virginia campaign. At the end of the war, Shields moved again, to Missouri, where he was again elected to the United States Senate.

John Mackay came to America at the height of the famine. After a short stay in New York, he moved on to California, where he took up prospecting and mining. In 1873 Mackay "struck it rich," when gold and silver deposits eventually valued at $200 million were discovered in his "Bonanza" mine.

Born hungry forty-two years earlier, John Mackay became a multimillionaire and one of California's first citizens. After a "glorious reign" in California, he returned to his port of entry, New York City, and established himself and his family in grand style. Mrs. Mackay

Thomas Fitzpatrick (above left), born in Ireland in 1799, was one of the earliest scouts on the American frontier. He often led army expeditions and wagon trains through uncharted land. Below the first wagon train over the Oregon Trail: the departure from St. Louis. Thomas Fitzpatrick was one of the leaders. General James Shields (above right), born in Ireland and elected a United States senator from three states, served his adopted country as a general in both the War with Mexico and the Civil War.

Left, the "Corduroy Trail" leading to Leadville, Colorado — home of the Unsinkable Molly Brown and her husband, "Leadville Johnny." This back-breaking trail, carved out of a hillside and paved with rough logs, was the entry point and supply route for mining pioneers like the Irish-American Browns. The legendary Mrs. John J. Brown (the Unsinkable Molly Brown) shown above with Captain A. H. Rostron, commander of the first ship to reach the survivors of the sunken Titanic. Molly Brown, who pioneered with her husband in the tough mining country of Colorado, showed her strength by rallying her lifeboat companions until Captain Rostron's ship arrived.

set out to conquer "polite society." Despite whispers about her "washerwoman" days, she succeeded in setting her family up in the "on its way up" style. Her daughter married into a titled European family.

Mackay's granddaughter made an even more interesting match. She married songwriter Irving Berlin.

Another wealthy Irish-American woman from the West who had her troubles with America's "polite society" was Margaret "Molly" Tobin Brown. Mrs. Brown happened to be returning from a European tour on the *Titanic* when that ship rammed an iceberg and sank. Her lifeboat companions later praised her performance amid the chaos. As she pulled her oar, Mrs. Brown lifted the survivors' spirits with a steady flow of jokes and songs.

"I'm unsinkable," "Molly" Brown told the press when she landed. Years later she was to be remembered in a Broadway musical and movie, *The Unsinkable Molly Brown*.

THE AMERICAN CIVIL WAR

War is a hideous and cruel experience, and civil war is more so. Men at war struggle for life on the most primitive level. It's them or us; it's him or me who will live. The American Civil War brought out the worst and the best in mankind. The Irish immigrants' role in this war was to provide much of both.

Although Daniel O'Connell would urge the Irish in America to support the abolition of slavery, the mass of the immigrants did not respond. The Irish were job-hungry and often competed with newly freed blacks for a limited number of jobs. Thus any sympathy they might feel was tempered by the burden of their own struggle for survival. Moreover, the immigrants distrusted the northern abolitionist groups. Why so much sympathy for the black man so far away, the Irish wondered, and no sympathy for the downtrodden immigrant so close to home? Some abolitionists often combined a deep concern for the slaves with bitter anti-Catholicism.

This antipathy to the black cause and to abolitionists, combined with resentment over a draft law that permitted a rich man to purchase his way out of the war, drove the Irish masses to bloody violence in 1863. The New York draft riots were the worst in the history of the city. Hundreds of thousands of dollars in damage was caused by looting and burning mobs. Hundreds of rioters were killed by the militia, but not before the mob had lynched several black men and set fire to the Colored Orphans Asylum.

Of course not all Irish rioted, nor were all the rioters Irish. Some of the Irish were on the police force and they stood by the law, "with the most exemplary gallantry," it was reported. Other Irish lined up with the rescuers at the orphanage. The priests, led by Archbishop John Hughes himself, worked to restore peace.

Perhaps one reason why the riot took hold in the Irish community was that so many of the good men, the natural responsible leaders, were off fighting for the Union. Over 150,000 Irish-born Americans answered President Abraham Lincoln's call for soldiers. Irish men and Irish regiments formed the front ranks at many of the most costly battles. At Fredricksburg, where Union soldiers were foolishly sent against a solidly entrenched foe, a no-doubt frustrated Confederate general yelled, "There are those dammed green flags again," as his own men cheered the shattered but still advancing Irish Brigade.

The "green flags" were those of the Massachusetts, New York, and Pennsylvania regiments, which formed the proudly named Irish Brigade. The kings of France had for centuries boasted of their brave Irish brigade made up of exiles, escaped rebels, and adventurers. Now Abraham Lincoln could boast of his brigade. "Never at Fontenoy, Albuera or at Waterloo was more undaunted courage displayed by the sons of Erin," wrote a British correspondent from inside the Confederate fortifications, "than during those six frantic dashes which they directed against the almost impregnable position of their foe...." Out of 1,300 men fielded by the brigade that day, 545 were killed, wounded, or missing by the following day.

Above, officers, their wives, and enlisted men of New York's Sixty-Ninth Regiment (one of the many Union-formed Irish regiments) gather for Sunday mass, probably at their field headquarters in Washington, D.C. Left, General Thomas Meagher. The immigrants called him "Meagher of the Sword" because of a famous speech he made in Ireland while a member of the rebellious "Young Ireland" movement. When the American Civil War erupted, he answered the call and rose quickly to the command of the famed Irish Brigade.

Above, a contemporary sketch of the New York City draft riots shows the rioters, who were largely Irish immigrants, holding a makeshift barricade against attacking federal troops. Below, Irish and German immigrants are being recruited into the Union Army as they enter the country. The billboard lists, in English and German, the cash bounties offered to persuade the penniless immigrants to enlist.

The brigade's general was Thomas F. Meagher. Meagher of the Sword, as the immigrants called him, was a one-time ally of O'Connell, who had been involved in the doomed Irish rising of 1848.

Everywhere in the Union army, on the casualty lists and on the honor lists, men like Meagher stepped out of Irish history and into American history. John Kavanagh, wounded in Ireland in 1848, was killed at the head of his company at Antietam. Joseph Burke of County Mayo, raised to be a British officer like his brothers, joined the rising of '48 and survived to command a brigade in the Army of the Cumberland. Michael Herbert, a veteran of the British army and the Papal Brigade, was killed in a Virginia pasture with the Irish Brigade.

Irish women also answered the Union call. One of these, "Irish Brigid" Divers, a nurse attached to the Michigan cavalry, was credited with rallying her retreating regiment at Fair Oaks, Virginia. "Arragh, go in b'ys," she cried, "and God be wid yez."

The Confederacy had its Irishmen, too, though not nearly so many, for the immigrants settled primarily in the North. Patrick Ronayne Cleburne, the "Stonewall Jackson of the West," as he was called, was one of these men. A veteran of the British army, he rose from captain to major general in the Confederate army, only to be killed in action in 1864. Sergeant Michael Sullivan, another Irish American in Confederate uniform, left his own lines and swam the Rappahannock River in order to return to Meagher one of the green flags lost at Fredricksburg. Then, with Meagher's permission and the assistance of some men of the brigade, Sullivan returned to his Georgia company.

"Know-Nothingism is dead," Meagher proclaimed in one of his great speeches during the war, and truly he was right. "The Irish soldier will henchforth take his stand by the side of the native born . . . and tell him that he has been equal to him in his allegiance to the Constitution."

Today, one of those "damn green flags" of the brigade is on display in the lobby of the Dail, the freely elected Parliament of the Republic of Ireland. It was brought to Ireland, as a gift from the American people, by President John Fitzgerald Kennedy.

THE IRISH IN POLITICS

In the years after the Civil War, the Irish were to make the Democratic party of the big cities their very own part of America. The Irish moved to conquer not Wall Street, not industry, but city hall. They built the urban political organization, shaped it to their needs, and in time adapted it to the needs of newer immigrant peoples.

When the famine Irish walked off those packet ships, the Democratic party was waiting to greet them. It was a party of friends ready to help. In those days there were no unemployment checks for those out of work, no social security pensions for older people, no free lunches for hungry schoolchildren. Government was mostly in the hands of those who believed that that government is best which governs least.

The immigrants needed an active government that would help them. They fashioned the Democratic party big-city "machine." Their objective was no high-minded goal of good government, no utopian vision of a great society; for the famine immigrants and the Irish who came after them, politics was simply a way of getting ahead in America.

"I chose politics," said James Michael Curley, son of famine immigrants, congressman, mayor of Boston, and governor of Massachusetts, "because the prospects of ever getting anywhere elsewhere seemed remote." John Fitzgerald, maternal grandfather of John Fitzgerald Kennedy and, like Curley, once mayor of Boston, went into politics "because an Irish boy could not get a job in any bank or a white collar job with a railroad."

The machine gave the immigrants what they needed — jobs, food, and clothing in tough times. And the immigrants responded with their votes. When the machine controlled city hall or the governor's mansion there was plenty of work for all. But even when the party was not in control of local government, the "bosses" continued to serve the people, with an eye toward the next election.

As the Irish fashioned it, the Democratic machine had continuity.

It was "*the* organ-eye-zation." Every member, from block captain or committeeman to county leader, had an understood and respected role. Promising men advanced up through these ranks, serving time, doing their part, until it was their turn to run, or to move up to the "bench," or to become a commissioner.

Of course, the machine was not always the helpful organization many of its supporters believed it to be. More than anything else, it was an instrument for seizing power — the power to run a city or a state — and in the battle for power in nineteenth-century America, the Irish made some rules of their own.

Memories of centuries of domination by English officials and English law had left the immigrants with a winking, skeptical attitude toward government. Congressman Timothy J. Campbell, born in County Cavan, once asked President Grover Cleveland for some favor that the president refused on the ground that it was unconstitutional. "Ah, Mr. President," Campbell is reported to have said, "what is the Constitution between friends?"

"Vote early and vote often" was one organization-man's battle plan. "Don't buy one more vote than you need" was the way another Irish-American boss put it.

Clearly the years of Irish control of the urban machines were not always marked by respectability or responsibility. Millions of dollars were stolen and millions more were wasted on frivolity. Endlessly ornate and often unnecessary public buildings were constructed just so that jobs would be available and graft would flow into the party treasury and the bosses' pockets. Street cleaning contracts would be signed, fees paid, men hired, and still the garbage would pile up. In some cities, the underworld and vice prospered because the bosses were busy elsewhere fighting political battles, or were just plain greedy.

Frequently during these years, business interests, church groups, and other reform-minded citizens got together in an attempt to "throw the rascals out." Sometimes the rascals were in fact thrown out — though they were often back in power by the next election. Sometimes the rascals were even caught with their hands in the public treasury, as happened in the case of William Marcy ("Boss") Tweed of New York's Tammany Hall Democratic Organization.

Tweed himself was not an Irishman, though his power certainly rested on his popularity with New York's Irish. One New York Irishman who did not admire Tweed, however, was Charles O'Connor, son of one of the exiles of '98, and the chief prosecutor at Tweed's trial. When Tweed left for jail in 1871, greatly mourned by the Irish, he was succeeded at Tammany by "Honest John" Kelly. Irish Americans were to run the Tammany Hall organization, and usually New York's City Hall, for the next half century.

"The Irish conquest of the cities" is one historian's caption for this time. In Chicago, Illinois, the bosses' names were "Hinky Dink" McKenna and "Bathhouse John" Coughlin; in Kansas City, Missouri, it was the Pendergast brothers; in Jersey City, New Jersey, it was Frank "I am the law" Hague; in Albany, New York, it was the O'Connell family.

America in these closing years of the nineteenth century was a country where seemingly insatiable robber barons battled each other for control of the nation's commerce and industry. "The public be damned" was one capitalist's slogan as he went his way ruthlessly amassing money and power.

Above left, Tammany leader Charles Murphy, wearing a Derby hat, poses in front of Tammany Hall. Boss Murphy and his followers prided themselves on adapting their machine to serve the needs of each new wave of immigrants. Center, President Woodrow Wilson pictured with his White House assistant, Irish-American Joseph P. Tumulty of New Jersey. Tumulty was one of the nation's outstanding politicians. He served as assistant and adviser when Wilson was governor of New Jersey and later when Wilson became President. Above right, The Honorable William Marcy Tweed, known as "Boss" Tweed. This American-born, Scots—Irish Protestant was extremely popular with New York City's Irish immigrants. While he stole millions from the public treasury (for which he was eventually jailed), he kept the immigrants content by supporting public building projects that provided the jobs they desperately needed. Below, an 1872 political leaflet in which James O'Brien, like many other Irish politicians, presents himself as a friend of the poor. Abraham Lawrence, O'Brien's opponent, is here charged with being the candidate of thieving Tammany Hall. The Indian was the nineteenth-century symbol of the New York City Democratic party of Tammany as it was then known. Tammany was a mythical Indian chief.

FOR MAYOR: JAMES O'BRIEN.

☞ Look on this Picture,

☞ And Look on This.

JAMES O'BRIEN, 1870.

I was hungry and he gave me food !

ABRAHAM R. LAWRENCE, APOLLO HALL, 1871.
Consistency thou art a Jewel.

ABRAHAM R. LAWRENCE, TAMMANY HALL, 1872.
Inconsistency art thou a Jewel ?

I was cold and he provided me with fuel.

Old Mortality Wm. F. Havemeyer, Age 100, Harlequin Candidate !

Against this background, the Irish bosses and their henchmen, while busily filling their pockets, saw themselves as merely managing their enterprise, their part of America, in a like manner.

"Jawn, niver steal a dure mat," advised "Mr. Dooley," the Irish philosopher and saloonkeeper created by newspaperman Finley Peter Dunne. "If ye do ye'll be invistigated, hanged an' maybe ray-formed. Steal a bank, me boy, steal a bank."

Yet, in the midst of all the thievery and roguery, despite the boon-doggling and the graft, the rascals, when they had a chance, advanced a simple social vision.

"My mother was obliged to work...as a scrubwoman toiling nights..." related James Michael Curley, many times mayor of Boston and a twice-convicted felon. "I thought of her one night while leaving City Hall during my first term as Mayor. I told the scrubwoman cleaning the corridors to get up; 'the only time a woman should go down on her knees is when she is praying to Almighty God' I said. Next morning I ordered long-handled mops and issued an order that scrubwomen were never again to get down on their knees in City Hall."

♣

ORGANIZING THE WORKINGMAN

How often do we see such paragraphs in the paper,
as an Irishman drowned —
an Irishman crushed by a beam —
an Irishman suffocated in a pit —
an Irishman blown to atoms by a steam engine —
ten, twenty Irishmen buried alive
by the sinking of a bank —
and other, like casualties and perils
to which honest Pat is constantly exposed,
in the hard toils for his daily bread.

These sad words are from an 1836 letter of an Irish immigrant. Seven years later Ralph Waldo Emerson wrote to Henry David Thoreau, telling of his discovery of "the poor Irish, who receives but sixty, or even fifty cents, for working from dark till dark...."

In 1846 Irish workers in New York organized and went on strike in an attempt to raise wages from 65 cents a day to 87½ cents a day. The strike was broken when the owners brought in immigrant German laborers who were eager for the 65 cents. Much the same happened during a New York dock strike by Irish workers in 1863, only at that time the strikebreakers were free black men.

In the Pennsylvania coal fields, a secret society of Irish miners known as "the Molly Maguires" erupted in the 1870s, trying to attain through bombings and sniping the wages and working conditions they had not attained through strikes. "The Mollies," who were a violent offshoot of the Ancient Order of Hibernians, were eventually broken up in 1875 when an informer named James McKenna infiltrated their ranks. Twenty "Mollies" were eventually hanged, solely on the testimony of their countryman, McKenna.

The Knights of Labor, founded in 1869 as a nationwide working-man's association, quickly became substantially Irish in membership. Terence Vincent Powderly, a Pennsylvania Irishman, was the organization's grand master workman during its most active years. Indeed, so many of the Knights were Irish that the Catholic church quickly became embroiled in a dispute over whether membership in the semisecret group should be prohibited because of the danger to a Catholic's faith and morals. "The idea [of labor organizations] is communistic" said one archbishop in 1875, "and no Catholic with any idea of the spirit of his religion will encourage them." Fortunately, the American workingman had a staunch Irish-American friend within the church, James Cardinal Gibbons, who worked tirelessly and successfully to prevent any ecclesiastical prohibition against union membership.

Although the Knights under Powderly were to achieve some significant strike victories, the organization began to disintegrate as a result of internal dissension. And as the Knights broke up, the American Federation of Labor grew apace under the leadership of a Dutch Jewish immigrant, Samuel Gompers; a Prussian immigrant, Adolph Strasser; and Peter J. McGuire, the son of famine immigrants.

Above, women delegates to the 1886 Knights of Labor convention. Below, a labor demonstration in 1871 promoting the eight-hour workday. The banner of P. J. McGuire's Carpenters Union appears in the sketch, a reminder that the movement was his idea. Right, an 1886 trolley-car-employees strike in New York City. Most of the strikers were Irish Americans, as were many of the police shown here trying to clear a path for a trolley.

JOHN O'DONNELL, RAILROAD COMMISSIONER.

YORKVILLE HARLEM

HARLEM 2ND AVE TO FULTON FERRY

McGuire, one labor historian states, "undoubtedly supplied what ideas the American Federation of Labor had for its foundation." It was he who first suggested "Labor Day" and he who promoted and organized the great labor campaign of the 1880s for the eight-hour workday. McGuire was a socialist. As he worked to build his own craft union, the Brotherhood of Carpenters and Joiners, the idea of workers controlling industry was his inspiration. But McGuire's vision was soon set aside. The Federation's goal was to be simply "more" — more money, more time off, more fringe benefits.

As the immigrants settled into American life, the father and sons often advanced from the insecure, backbreaking toil of day laborers to work in skilled trades like carpentry and plumbing. These men were the backbone of the union-organizing drives of the nineteenth century. Once their unions were organized, however, the great mass of Irish Americans tended to play a moderate if not conservative role. No doubt the antisocialist preaching of the church helped to dampen the socialist movement in the largely Irish Federation.

McGuire died in 1906, a tired and unfulfilled man, but still loyal to the workingman's cause. "I've got to get to California, the boys in Local 22 need me," were the last words P. J. had left behind.

THE IMMIGRANT BARDS

The Irish had always regarded theater and the related spoken arts as very serious enterprises. In ancient times, the kingdoms of Ireland were governed by an elaborate system of laws, based upon custom and interpreted by a legal class called the brehons. When these laws were violated, the brehons often turned for enforcement or punishment to an unlikely source — the bards. These traveling poets, or minstrels, had the power of satire and ridicule. Protected by the well-established custom of the land, they fearlessly turned their talents against the lawbreaker, no matter how high or mighty. Words, and the ability to sing them well, were power.

Down through the centuries, the Irish continued to value the "music maker" and the man with a "gift of gab." In times of oppression, words became a way of saying "yes" to a conqueror while meaning "no" or "never." Queen Elizabeth I confronted just such a man in Lord Cormac Carthy of Blarney, who regularly said "yes" but always delayed fulfilling his promises. "This is all Blarney," the queen protested. "What he says he never means."

Illiteracy among the great mass of peasants only reinforced this respect and instinct for words. Immigrants were, as in so many other things, true Irishmen in their devotion to spoken poetry and the theater. The theater was a place to go after a hard week, a place where fantastic talk provoked teary visions of the Old Country. Inside the walls of New York's Park Theatre or Novelty Hall or any one of the other showplaces that specialized in Irish entertainment, the immigrants would be stirred by tales of ancient kings and heroes. Dreary lives would be uplifted for a night, or even days, by uproarious comedies featuring a classic character, "the stage Irishman."

Edward ("Ned") Harrigan and Tony Hart were the "hottest ticket" of those days, writing, producing and acting in a seemingly endless list of plays about immigrant life in New York. Harrigan called his plays "knock down and slambang" theater. The largely immigrant audiences loved them. In more than one play he had the ceiling cave in on stage; in one scene, a boat exploded; in another, he arranged for a real bonfire. Often, Harrigan closed a scene with an on-stage cyclone or thunderstorm, bringing the curtain down amid riotous cheers.

John Boyle O'Reilly was the immigrants' poet laureate — and more. A man of action as well as of words, O'Reilly first came to the attention of the immigrants when he was sentenced to death by the English in 1866. O'Reilly had been a British soldier and at the same time a subversive agent for rebellious Irish forces. Not surprisingly, the British government accused him of treason.

The death sentence was commuted and after a term in an English prison, O'Reilly was transported to a penal colony in Australia. By 1869, O'Reilly had escaped aboard an American ship and arrived to a hero's reception in the United States. He was to stay there, thinking, writing, and plotting until his death in 1890.

Left, Tony Hart (l.) and Ned Harrigan (r.) in a scene from Ireland V. Italia. Like other Harrigan and Hart productions, this play portrayed life among New York's immigrants in a rough, rowdy, but affectionate manner. Above, this sketch of an 1899 play, The Marquis of Steyne, shows Irish actor Tyrone Power on stage. Power's son and namesake was to become a well-known Irish-American movie star during the next century.

His life-long devotion to the cause of the oppressed Irish gave him the power to speak to and for other oppressed peoples. When Boston dedicated a memorial to Crispus Attucks, the free black man who had been killed in the Boston Massacre, O'Reilly was called on for a poem:

Call it riot or revolution, his hand first
clenched at the crown;
His feet were the first in perilous place to
pull the king's flag down;
His breast was the first one rent apart that
liberty's stream might flow;
For our freedom now and forever, his head
was the first laid low.

♣

A BOLD FENIAN

Soldiers are we, whose lives
are pledged to Ireland.
Some have come from a
land beyond the wave.

Lines from *The Soldier's Song*,
National Anthem of Ireland
by Peadar Kearney
(1883–1942)

Much of the support that enabled Irish patriots to remain constant to their goal of a free Ireland came from "a land beyond the wave," the United States. So great was Irish-American support for Ireland, that at one point the London *Times* commented, "The Irish question has become an Irish-American question."

In 1858, men acting in Ireland and the United States set up the two branches of what was to become known as the Fenian Brotherhood. With a name derived from the Gaelic, this Irish and Irish-American organization began immediately to plan for insurrection in Ireland. American Fenians were advised to join the Union army to prepare themselves for war service in the Old Country.

The first phase of the Fenian campaign was an 1866 attack across the Vermont border into Canada by 800 Irish-American Civil War veterans organized as the "Right Wing of the Army of Ireland." The assault, an attempt to take English territory to bargain with for Ireland, was unsuccessful.

The rising took place in Ireland in 1867. Among "the bold Fenian men" were substantial numbers of returned Irish Americans. The rising was unsuccessful, due largely to the efforts of informers, but the pattern for Irish and Irish-American cooperation was set. The Atlantic became a highway for Irish conspirators.

One of busiest Irish-American conspirators was John Devoy, a veteran of both the French Foreign Legion and the Fenian Brotherhood. In "the refuge of exiles," America, Devoy wasted not a moment in organizing his fellow Irish Americans to work and scheme for the freedom of the Old Country.

Devoy busied himself through the years around the turn of the century with one or another nationalist scheme. In 1914 the level of conspiracy peaked when World War I, pitting England against Germany, erupted in Europe. With one hand Devoy organized Irish Americans in a campaign to keep the United States out of this war. With the other he negotiated with the German government for arms and ammunition to arm the Irish rebels of 1916. President Woodrow Wilson, furious with Devoy and his allies, like New York Judge Dan Cohalan, referred to them derisively as "hyphenated-Americans."

New York City in 1871 was very much an Irish city in spirit, if not in fact. When a group of exiles from the Irish revolutionary organization — the Fenians — arrived on tour, a City Hall reception and parade was a popular event. This procession (above) honoring the Irish rebels took place on February 9. Fenian leader John Devoy (right) pictured here with Eamon DeValera (second from left), American-born participant in Ireland's 1916 rising against England, and later president of a free Ireland. Also pictured are Judge Daniel Cohalan (left) and Judge John Goff (second from right), long-time supporters of the Irish cause.

When America entered the war, Irish Americans, as ever before, responded to the call for volunteers. And when it was over, these same people watched closely when Wilson sat down with the victorious allied prime ministers to set up the League of Nations. Irish independence was not provided for by the League treaty as Devoy and others were quick to note. Following Devoy's lead, in the 1920 presidential election the Irish-American community voted against the treaty, and against the pro-treaty Democrats.

The London *Times* obituary on the occasion of Devoy's death in 1929 called him a "most bitter and persistent, as well as most dangerous enemy of this country." Devoy would have loved the compliment. By that time Ireland had made giant strides toward independence because of "Bold Fenians" like Devoy.

THE FIGHTING IRISH

Advancement in most professions was limited by prejudice against the Irish and by their own lack of education. Like many other ethnic groups that came after them, they too broke into the American mainstream via sports.

The Irish of the nineteenth century admired a man who could use his hands. John L. Sullivan, "The Boston Strong Boy," grandson of an Ireland-born fighting champion, fit the bill. In those bare-knuckle boxing days, Sullivan defeated a list of heavyweights, mostly Irish, from Tom Scannel of Boston to Paddy Ryan, "the Troy Terror," to Jake Kilrain. The Kilrain fight lasted seventy-five rounds and ended only when the challenger dropped from exhaustion. From 1877 to 1892, the great John L. took on all challengers and, whether the fight was with bareknuckles or with gloves, he bested all of them. "The Pride of Boston" received presidential headlines and enthu-

John L. Sullivan fights Jake Kilrain in New Orleans.

WASHINGTON BASE BALL CLUB.

WASHINGTON.

0169. Carroll, Second Base, Washington. GOODWIN & CO., NEW YORK.
0170. Kreig, First Base, Washington. GOODWIN & CO., NEW YORK.
0163. Whitney, Pitcher, Washington. GOODWIN & CO., NEW YORK.
0191. Gaffney, Manager of Washington Club. GOODWIN & CO., NEW YORK.
0158. Dealy, Catcher, Washington. GOODWIN & CO., NEW YORK.
0161. Dealy, Catcher, Washington. GOODWIN & CO., NEW YORK.

0161. Dealy, Catcher, Washington. GOODWIN & CO., NEW YORK.
0179. Hines, Centre Field, Washington. GOODWIN & CO., NEW YORK.
0197. Myers, Short Stop, Washington. GOODWIN & CO., NEW YORK.
0125. Crane, Second Base, Washington. GOODWIN & CO., NEW YORK.
0126. Mack, Catcher, Washington. GOODWIN & CO., NEW YORK.
0189. Farrell, Second Base, Washington. GOODWIN & CO., NEW YORK.

0231. Carroll, Left Field, Washington. GOODWIN & CO., NEW YORK.
0178. Hines, Centre Field, Washington. GOODWIN & CO., NEW YORK.
0185. Shoch, Right Field, Washington. GOODWIN & CO., NEW YORK.
0127. Mack, Catcher, Washington. GOODWIN & CO., NEW YORK.
0189. Farrell, Second Base, Washington. GOODWIN & CO., NEW YORK.
0162. Whitney, Pitcher, Washington. GOODWIN & CO., NEW YORK.

0170. Kreig, First Base, Washington. GOODWIN & CO., NEW YORK.
0200. Carroll, Left Field, Washington. GOODWIN & CO., NEW YORK.
0193. Donnelly, Third Base, Washington. GOODWIN & CO., NEW YORK.
0157. Dealy, Catcher, Washington. GOODWIN & CO., NEW YORK.
0160. Dealy, Catcher, Washington. GOODWIN & CO., NEW YORK.
0173. O'Day, Pitcher, Washington. GOODWIN & CO., NEW YORK.

siastic crowds. And the phrase "I shook the hand that shook the hand of John L. Sullivan" became part of American lore. In 1892, after almost fifteen years of fighting and celebrating, John L. was defeated by a San Francisco Irish American, "Gentleman Jim" Corbett.

In the twentieth century Irishmen like Gene Tunney and Jack Dempsey were to continue the John L. tradition. Indeed, Irish Americans were to remain so dominant in this sport that often non-Irish boxers took Irish "ring" names to persuade the fans that they too were "tough."

At this time the emerging sport of baseball was also filled with Irish names, and not all of them belonged to Irishmen. The prominence of Irish Americans in the early days of baseball was so accepted that Ernest Thayer did the popular thing when he titled his poetic tale of a mighty slugger "Casey at the Bat." "Slide, Kelly, Slide" was everybody's favorite song for a while, and Michael ("King") Kelly, a famous base stealer, was the reason.

Charles Comiskey ("the Old Roman"), a son of famine immigrants, broke into professional baseball as a first baseman with the St. Louis Browns in 1881. He immediately began to have an impact on the game to which he was to devote fifty years. Unlike all other first basemen before him, Comiskey played off the bag and first basemen ever since have followed his lead.

By 1900, Comiskey was not only a player, he was also an executive in the increasingly organized sport. With a few other executives, including another Irish-American player-manager named Cornelius McGillicuddy ("Connie Mack"), Comiskey participated in organizing the American League. Both Mack and Comiskey became "grand old men of baseball." Comiskey finished his career in 1931 as owner of the Chicago White Sox; Mack finished his as president of the Philadelphia Athletics, after leading the team to eight league championships in his fifty years as manager.

The Washington Baseball Club featured on Old Judge Cigarettes Baseball Cards — 1887. Irish Americans predominate: Farrell, Gaffney, O'Day, and a catcher named Mack. Cornelius McGillicuddy, or Connie Mack, became the "grand old man of baseball."

The first major league All Star Game in 1933 was an all-Irish managers' battle — Connie Mack of the American League against John McGraw of the National. "Muggsy" McGraw, as he was known when he was an outstanding third baseman with the Baltimore Orioles at the turn of the century, became the "Little Napoleon" during his thirty years managing the New York Giants. In those McGraw years, the Giants took ten pennants and three world championships. As impressive as McGraw's record is, manager Joe McCarthy's record is even more so — nine pennants in two leagues and seven world championships with the New York Yankees.

When people today think of Irish Americans in sports, they usually think first of Notre Dame University's football team, "the fighting Irish." Strangely enough, "the fighting Irish" have not always been very Irish. The team first came to national attention in 1913 when two honorary "fighting Irishmen," Gus Dorais and Knute Rockne, used a revolutionary tactic — the forward pass — to humble a strong West Point team. Rockne returned to Notre Dame to coach the outstanding teams of the 1920s.

The Modern Era

MOVING UP

In the early years of the twentieth century, throughout the country, the Irish were "moving up." American-born sons and daughters raised in relative comfort were moving out of the old neighborhoods, working in banks, voting Republican, and forgetting about the hard days. Fathers who worked in blue-collared work shirts watched their sons put on white shirts and go to work without lunchpails.

Those who were born in the hard time of the famine were mostly gone, as were the veterans of the Irish Brigade. Most of the No Irish Need Apply signs had been taken down and anti-Catholic political movements did not seem as threatening. The time when most Irish were immigrants was past and a new era was at hand. The Irish who had lived in old shacks or slums had given way to those able to afford a better life. These newly secure Irish, quick to adopt genteel middle-class styles, were called "lace curtain" Irish.

Historian Thomas Beer recorded that during the Spanish-American War, a group of young journalists went looking for the first American soldier to top the enemy fortifications on San Juan Hill. The newspapermen were convinced (wrongly) he would be a red-haired Irishman. In two previous wars, men had publicly doubted whether the Irish would fight for America. How things had changed!

There was to be no need for an Irish Brigade in the twentieth

Above, an Irish-American family at turn of the century — moving up. Father and mother were immigrants from County Kerry. One of the sons pictured here was killed in World War II; another became an engineer and retired recently from a high post in city government; another became a policeman; and another a bus driver. One daughter became a schoolteacher; another a secretary; and another combined marriage with a successful career in the federal civil service. Below, "What Mrs. McCarthy says," according to this Kirkman's Soap ad of 1892, is, "I always use Kirkman's Soap." The public image of the Irish woman as a domestic servant or washerwoman, was as generally accepted in these times as the stereotype of the rowdy, good-natured, drinking Irish male.

century. The Irish no longer had to prove themselves whenever the terrible call to war sounded. Immigrants and their sons filled in the ranks shoulder to shoulder with their fellow Americans.

The process of moving up caused some changes in Irish attitudes toward both American society and themselves. The native American establishment changed its mind about the Irish; and the Irish were just as surely changing their minds about the establishment. Now they were becoming concerned with being "accepted." No more the raucous, drunken boyo's; no more the dreamers of dreams.

Ned Harrigan once summed up the Irish he knew in an anecdote; it seems that an undertaker, after preparing the deceased for burial, took a long look at Pat's remains and wondered, "He doesn't look right. He just doesn't look natural." Says Mike looking on, "Why don't ye paint a black eye on him?"

The wild Irish, the brawling, rowdy Irish who could once laugh at such a story about themselves, were now policemen, bank clerks, nurses, insurance salesmen, teachers, and accountants. Such stories would no longer do. For these people, "the stage Irishman" had become an insulting, degrading stereotype.

The new Irish Americans instead preferred the happy-go-lucky, patriotic fare of a man like George M. Cohan. The grandson of immigrants from County Cork who spelled the name "Keohane," George M. practically began life onstage. His parents were in vaudeville and when he and his sister came along, father Jerry just expanded the act.

As a performer, Cohan presented a different version of the stage Irishman. Instead of wearing "tatters," this man was dapper; this man didn't play the buffoon for laughs, instead he wisecracked. In Cohan's plays and songs, the Irish became charming and likeable. The children of parents who once cheered Harrigan's "slambang" theater now applauded Cohan's light musicals.

Left, the statue of George M. Cohan on Broadway, New York City. In the back of it there is another Broadway statue honoring another Irish American — Father Duffy, chaplain to New York's Sixty-Ninth Regiment, "The Fighting Irish," in World War I. Above right, George M. Cohan, as played by another Irish American, James Cagney, in this Hollywood film version of Cohan's life, Yankee Doodle Dandy. *Below right, Pat Rooney, a nineteenth-century Irish-American actor, in costume as the "stage Irishman."*

As the stereotype stage Irishman passed out of existence, other Irish-American stereotypes gained popular acceptance. The Irish cop was one. Now the always pugnacious Irishman could be pugnacious and still remain on the side of law and order.

In Ireland during these years, the curtain rose on the final act of the long drama of rebellion. On Easter Sunday in 1916, a group of poets, journalists, and workmen proclaimed Ireland a republic and seized British government installations in Dublin. The rising lasted barely a week but the spirit of rebellion was fueled once again. When the British executed a number of the Republican rebels, thousands of Irish men and women stepped forward in their place. A long, bloody guerrilla war began.

The American Irish provided vigorous support for the rebel cause during this time. Candidates seeking Irish votes were wise to pledge themselves to Ireland's cause and donate generously at fund-raising events, or else the Irish would vote "no" en masse. This was the time when John Devoy and others tried to buy German arms and smuggle them into Ireland. Although the Irish were settling into America, they had not forgotten the Old Country and "the old fight."

LATTER-DAY BARDS

In twentieth-century America, a new generation of Irish bards came of age. These latter-day men and women put aside the minstrel's harps and the music hall productions. They turned to modern forms of expression like the novel, legitimate theater, and motion picture.

Novelists like F. Scott Fitzgerald, John O'Hara, and James T. Farrell are regarded as being among the best American writers in this century. These men demonstrated their Irish inheritance in a variety of ways. Fitzgerald and O'Hara both wrote about the rich and privileged in America with the keen awareness of an outsider seeing something for the first time. And as Irish Americans, they were "outsiders" in privileged America.

Farrell's novels, on the other hand, like the classic *Studs Lonigan* and the Danny O'Neill series, are about ordinary Irish Americans. They are written from inside the community and are about the battle to get out and become part of the greater world.

Eugene O'Neill, considered by many to be the finest American playwright, was the son of famine immigrant and actor James O'Neill. Young O'Neill's Irish background figures prominently in many of his stage masterpieces. In *Long Day's Journey Into Night*, perhaps his greatest play, O'Neill puts his own family on stage to act out roles drawn directly from the Irish experience in America.

"The critics have missed the most important thing about me and my work," this Nobel Prize-winning dramatist once said, "the fact that I am Irish."

A distant cousin of O'Neill, Jean Kerr is today one of Broadway's most successful and popular playwrights. Kerr, however, is a humorist who creates wit-filled family battles. Her point of view is that of an assimilated suburbanized Catholic. Though the child of immigrant parents, Kerr's writing touches only occasionally and incidentally on the Irish and their ways. But as she stops to look at the Irish with her sharp eye, Ms. Kerr hits the target. When she writes about sophisticated, modern Americans, who occasionally seem Irish, the point she is making is that the Irish are almost gone. Like herself, they are mostly assimilated and at home in America.

While the writers were putting their visions onto paper, another Irish-American bard was telling his tales in a new, totally modern form, the film. Sean O'Feeney, born in Maine in 1895 of immigrant parents, was by 1917 directing his first movie in Hollywood, and using a new name — John Ford. Despite the name change, however, Ford never denied his Irishness. Indeed if his pictures are taken as evidence, Ford gloried in being an Irish American.

The Informer was a Liam O'Flaherty novel about a traditional Irish villain, the man who turns in his "rebel" friends for silver. Turned into a film classic by Ford, it earned the director his first Academy Award. Ford followed *The Informer* with other explicitly Irish films like *The Plough and the Stars* in 1937; *The Quiet Man*, another Academy Award-winner in 1952; and *The Last Hurrah* in 1958. This last film, a sentimental tale of a ruthless but appealing Irish politician, is a loving portrait by Ford of his own people.

Ford's Irish films are only a small portion of his stunning creative output. Beginning in 1924 with *The Iron Horse,* he soon became Hollywood's predominant director of westerns.

The U.S. Cavalry, as John Ford re-created it in his westerns, and as it actually was, is full of Irishmen. In *Fort Apache,* an immigrant sergeant dies in the great battle while his West Point-educated son lives to fight on. In *Rio Grande* and *She Wore a Yellow Ribbon,* Victor McLaglen portrays the boisterous, brawny Sgt. Quincannon. At one point in *Rio Grande* Quincannon slips into an abandoned church to rescue children captured by Indians. As the battle rages outside, Quincannon, like a true Irishman, pauses in the hurried escape long enough to genuflect before the altar. John Ford knew his people.

The list of other Irish Americans in the creative arts is almost endless — novelists like J. F. Powers, Flannery O'Connor, and Tom McHale; playwrights like Philip Barry and George Kelly; writers Jimmy Breslin, Pete Hamill, and Joe Flaherty. Breslin, in particular, has captured a national audience with his recent novel, *World Without End, Amen,* which contrasts today's Irish in America with their oppressed cousins in Northern Ireland. Sometimes all this "talking" must weigh heavily on our fellow Americans. But it's all part of being Irish.

From top left: television personality and newspaper columnist, Ed Sullivan; playwright Jean Kerr (born Brigid Jean Collins in Scranton, Pa.). Her latest play, Finishing Touches, *played to full houses on Broadway after its successful opening in 1973; writer Jimmy Breslin. His ironic tale of an Irish-American policeman who goes to Ireland shows that the bardic tradition is alive and well in Queens County, New York City; Eileen Farrell — internationally-known former star of the Metropolitan Opera. She is the daughter of Michael and Catherine Kennedy Farrell, known professionally as the Singing O'Farrells; Eugene O'Neill — Nobel Prize-winning Irish-American playwright; lower left, Irishman Gypo Nolan (played by Victor McLaglen) offers his condolences to the mother and the sister of the man he secretly betrayed in this scene from John Ford's Academy Award-winner,* The Informer. *Over the centuries, so many Irish rebellions and rebels were betrayed by informers, that the word and the role have a uniquely distasteful meaning for all Irish.*

THE QUEST — THE IRISH FROM SMITH TO KENNEDY

In a St. Patrick's Day edition of *The Carolina Israelite,* Harry Golden summed up the story of the Irish in America: "Those who were told they couldn't apply for a job now have *the* job." He was, of course, talking about the election of John Fitzgerald Kennedy to the presidency. The journey to the White House had begun over a century earlier in the famine days. But the pace quickened in the twentieth century with the appearance of a man affectionately called "the Happy Warrior," Alfred E. Smith.

In the slangy way he talked, the dapper way he dressed, and the devout Catholic way he worshiped, Smith revealed a kinship with his immigrant ancestors and with other Irish Americans like himself who were still struggling to find a place in their country. Al Smith's political career began in the usual Irish-American fashion — he was a Tammany-elected New York Assemblyman. But he was no ordinary Tammany hack. He was conscientious, hard-working, and a progressive. In time he won the respect of even anti-Tammany reformers. And, when he ran successfully for governor of New York, both bosses and reformers were among his supporters.

Once in the governor's mansion, Smith set about passing a full agenda of progressive social legislation. There was more money for education. Factory working conditions were improved. Housing development was initiated. The state bureaucracy was reorganized and streamlined. New public parks and beaches, as well as new roads, were opened. And through it all, though the "bosses" were often eagerly right beside him, there was not even a hint of significant graft.

In 1928 Smith received the Democratic party's presidential nomination and inched closer to "the job" than any Irish American before him. But he was to get no farther. When the election totals were in, Smith was defeated, largely because the country was prosperous. After eight years of Republican presidents, a people who thought they saw prosperity all around them were not likely to vote for change. In addition, there was plenty of evidence of anti-Catholic rumor-mongering and an anti-Catholic vote throughout the country. Many Catholics wondered: could there ever be a Catholic president?

With the stock market crash of 1929 and the Great Depression that followed, men and women throughout the country desperately looked for work. Breadlines formed in the streets outside Salvation Army missions as people too hungry to be embarrassed waited for a handout. Riots broke out in many cities. And from the White House came only more talk about prosperity — the kind of talk that had defeated Al Smith.

The Great Depression struck at the Irish in a significant way. Most of them were no longer immigrants, but first- and second-generation Americans. For many of them the long journey from the slums to middle-class stability was about to end just as the Depression hit.

One man the Irish turned to for answers at this time was a radio priest, Father Coughlin, whose Sunday evening broadcasts were one of the nation's most listened-to programs. At first Coughlin spoke only on religious themes, but as the depression grew more severe, he turned to politics and economics. Coughlin's combination of vague antiwealth populism with priestly appeals to greater Christian charity sounded "right" to millions of depression-stunned Americans. His sermons, of course, had a special appeal to the Irish because he was a priest.

Another man the Irish turned to was Franklin Delano Roosevelt. Though disappointed that the Democratic presidential nominee in 1932 was F.D.R. and not their beloved Al Smith, the Irish across the country turned out for the Democrats once again. And once in the White House, Roosevelt turned to a number of Irish Americans for advice and assistance.

One man who made it his business to have F.D.R. elected and reelected was James A. Farley. When Franklin D. Roosevelt was elected governor of New York in 1928, Farley was beside him as state Democratic chairman. And when F.D.R. was reelected in 1930, Farley began Roosevelt's campaign for the 1932 presidential nomination.

Claiming that he was merely visiting friends, Jim Farley crossed and criss-crossed the country during those years lining up the needed Democratic convention votes for Roosevelt. His style was direct, friendly, and meticulous. Everyone he met, everyone, got a personalized letter, reminding them of the occasion, and of F.D.R. It was signed in green ink by "Jim."

When Roosevelt went to the White House in 1933, Farley went along. He was to serve F.D.R. until 1940 as postmaster-general, Democratic party national chairman, and all-round political manager. It was Farley who had to make sure that voters regularly pulled down the Democratic lever.

Also in the White House was a brilliant young lawyer from Rhode Island, Thomas ("Tommy the Cork") Corcoran. In the Senate, F.D.R. could look to men like Joseph O'Mahoney of Wyoming, a son of immigrants, and an anti-big-business progressive. In the House of Representatives, Irish Americans who supported F.D.R.'s New Deal programs were plentiful. John McCormack of Boston was one of the most faithful.

Among the Fenians who invaded Canada in 1866 was one Irish rebel whose son was to serve as F.D.R.'s attorney-general and then to be appointed a justice of the United States Supreme Court. Red-headed Frank Murphy was sworn in as governor of Michigan in 1937 just in time to face the great auto workers' sit-down strikes. Not long before, other American officials had called out troops to break these strikes, but Murphy respected the workers rights and chose the calmer course of vigorous negotiation. As with a number of other Irish-American leaders of this time, Murphy's outspoken sympathy for working people was fueled by a basic, religious concept of justice.

Defeated in his bid for reelection as governor, Murphy then went to Washington as attorney-general. There he distinguished himself again, actively prosecuting a number of well-known criminals and shady politicians of both parties. He also created the Civil Rights Division within the Department of Justice, which became a vital instrument in securing full rights for black Americans.

Soon F.D.R. had another job for the Michigan "red-head" — associate justice of the United States Supreme Court. Murphy's years on the Supreme Court were apparently not happy ones for he was basically a doer and an activist. But even so, he excelled again. When the Supreme Court upheld the World War II decision forcibly to relocate thousands of Japanese Americans in detention centers, Murphy passionately and convincingly dissented.

At one point in his career, Murphy had been sent by Roosevelt to court that other Michigan Irish-Catholic, Father Coughlin. Murphy was not successful.

Above, two Irish Americans, Governor Alfred E. Smith of New York (front row, right) and New York City Mayor James Walker (front row, second from left) pictured in 1929 at the cornerstone-laying ceremony for the new Tammany Hall. The others are various Tammany officers. Left, the radio priest, Father Charles Coughlin of Michigan. His Sunday evening broadcasts drew huge audiences throughout the country and made the outspoken priest politically powerful. At one time, he supported Democratic President Franklin D. Roosevelt, but by 1936 he was promoting his own party, the Union party, and his own presidential candidate, Congressman William Lemke.

In 1936, after years of both praising and denouncing Roosevelt, Coughlin set up his own Union party and nominated Congressman William Lemke for president. The radio priest, the Irish might say, had been "carried away by the sound of his voice." Lemke lost badly, getting less than a million votes while F.D.R. polled 27 million and Republican Alfred Landon 16 million. Coughlin barely paused for breath before he was back on the airwaves again.

But something had happened in the disastrous Lemke campaign. Coughlin in his new role of stumping politician had let his rhetoric run away from him, even more than usual. F.D.R., he would tell various audiences, was a "liar," "communistic," and "anti-God." The choice between Roosevelt and Landon was a choice "between carbolic acid and rat poison." Harsh words these were, especially from a priest. Coughlin soon got into the habit of taking off his priest's collar while campaigning. Irish Catholics and many others were quick to take note of this symbolic step-down and to take offense.

The public decline of Coughlin quickened after Lemke's loss. Soon he was flirting with anti-Semitism both on the air and in his writings. Coughlin had always paid his bills for air time by appealing for public contributions. By 1940, the contributions had stopped. The nation had turned him off.

Another Irish-American churchman, this one a frequent visitor to Capitol Hill and the White House, was the archbishop of New York City, Francis Spellman. In 1939, Spellman was appointed to the post that immigrant Archbishop John Hughes had held in the turbulent days of the Know-Nothings. Like his predecessors, Archbishop Spellman was to be an outspoken advocate of Catholic interests.

Jim Farley left the White House at this time after guiding F.D.R. through two stunningly successful election campaigns. Farley now wanted to try for "*the* job," but he got no farther than a few votes at the 1940 Democratic convention. The renominated Roosevelt now turned to a new manager, a new-style boss from the Bronx, Edward J. Flynn.

Through these first eight years of Roosevelt's presidency, one Irish American stood out. Joseph P. Kennedy was a rare man, a self-made multimillionaire who invaded some castles that had never before housed an Irishman. He went to Harvard at a time when

Mayor James Michael Curley announced to cheers that his son would rather go to a Catholic college. Although banking was definitely not an Irish business, Kennedy became the nation's youngest bank president at twenty-six. He made millions on Wall Street, out-thinking men whose families had run American finance for generations. And he made more millions in motion picture production, a field where the only previous Irish figures were actors or directors, not financial organizers.

F.D.R. turned to this man whose grandfather had been an immigrant, and whose father was a politician and bar owner, and asked him to run the newly created Securities and Exchange Commission. Kennedy was being given the power to regulate the nation's major financial institutions. He took the job and once again demonstrated his capabilities.

In 1938, the president sent Joe Kennedy to Great Britain as the American ambassador. Again Kennedy passed the test. As World War II came closer to Britain, Kennedy became convinced that the island nation could not meet the challenge of Nazi Germany. When he advised conciliation, many people felt he was urging appeasement of Hitler. Kennedy's condemnation of fascism was as sincere and forthright as any man's, but he calculated the chances for victory as low and urged caution on America. F.D.R. disagreed and the men were never close allies again.

When war came, the Irish responded as before. Ireland, now an independent nation, chose to remain neutral in this war and though some bigots tried to stir up anti-Irish feelings, the attempt was feeble. The Irish were too much a part of America now to be doubted. Joseph Kennedy saw three sons and a British son-in-law go to war. Only two sons returned.

After the war, the Irish as a group picked up right about where they were at the time of the Great Depression. Postwar prosperity touched most of them and once again the hard days seemed far behind.

Politicking began almost at once. Joe Kennedy's oldest surviving son, John Fitzgerald Kennedy, returned from the war a hero and promptly ran for Congress. He was elected and reelected for each term thereafter until 1952, when he announced his candidacy for the U.S. Senate.

Young Kennedy won again and once more, for the first time in years, people began to talk of an Irish Catholic in the White House. Kennedy's 1952 opponent, Yankee Henry Cabot Lodge, had expected to receive vital support from a Republican Irish-American senator, Joseph R. McCarthy of Wisconsin. But McCarthy stayed away from Massachusetts that year.

Senator McCarthy, like Father Coughlin, was an Irish American who built up a large national following at a time when America was in a state of discontent. In the years following World War II, Americans were prosperous but still ill at ease. Soviet Russia, an ally in the hot war with Nazi Germany, had quickly become a cold-war enemy. Around the globe, the Russian Communist government and its agents seemed intent upon extending their own control and diminishing American influence. In the United States the American Communist party defended the Soviet foreign expansion. Many Americans watched angrily. A number of celebrated court trials and congressional investigations provided some evidence that Soviet supporters were busy spying and plotting against the United States. The nation grew angrier.

In 1950 the Korean War began. Soviet-aided North Korea invaded South Korea. American soldiers were soon battling Korean and Chinese Communist troops in a bitter, stalemated war. Across the United States, frustrated, angry people — many Irish among them — began to listen to the senator from Wisconsin who said he knew who the spies were. Often he displayed lists of government employees whom he called "card-carrying Communists" or "security risks."

There were, of course, just enough real party members or quietly active Soviet apologists around to make McCarthy's charges ring true. But frequently he attacked with little or no real evidence. He

Top, Justice Frank Murphy of the United States Supreme Court. As governor of Michigan, his handling of the auto-workers strikes in 1937 earned him respect and distinction. When Murphy was attorney general of the United States, he created the Civil Rights Division in the Justice Department. Alfred Smith (left) listens intently as Governor Herbert Lehman and Francis Cardinal Spellman talk. To the Cardinal's left is Monsignor Lavelle and then New York City Mayor Fiorello La Guardia.

identified as Soviet agents people whose political beliefs he did not like or did not understand. At one point, McCarthy identified former chairman of the Joint Chiefs of Staff and Secretary of State George Marshall as a member of "a great conspiracy," a charge even the senator's friends disputed. McCarthy, always on the attack, was quick to label his critics, whether professors, clergymen, or newspapers, as "procommunist."

McCarthy was an Irish American and he was looked upon as one by most Americans. The Irish, always Catholic, had been consistently hostile to atheistic communism, even when the Soviets were America's fighting allies in World War II. Now, many Irish believed McCarthy was publicly proving them right while dramatically demonstrating, once again, Irish loyalty to the United States.

In time, McCarthy's baseless attacks convinced many people that the senator was only serving his own hunger for publicity and power. These Americans saw that McCarthy's anticommunism did not distinguish between Communists and liberal reformers. It did not distinguish between well-motivated error and treason. It was to them basically subversive and un-American.

In 1954, the United States Senate by a vote of sixty-seven to twenty-two censured Joseph McCarthy for his activities.

Other Irish Americans practiced a kind of anticommunism that was different from McCarthy's. For them it was not simply a matter of effective internal security arrangements. First of all, it was to correct the faults of American society and to better the lives of Americans. One Irish American who belongs to this group is labor leader George Meany.

George Meany was born in the Bronx, in New York City, son of a plumber's union official and grandson of an immigrant. He left high school to become a plumber's apprentice, received his plumber's card at twenty-two, and by his twenty-eighth year was business agent for a plumbers' union. Meany has been working for the workingman ever since. Today he is president of the American Federation of Labor-Congress of Industrial Organizations (AFL-CIO), the unified voice of the labor movement in the United States.

Under Meany, the AFL-CIO has become a powerful force in Washington, fighting for progressive legislation. Labor's influence is exerted on a broad list of legislative proposals from health care in-

Above left, Senator Joseph McCarthy of Wisconsin pictured in a typical situation, preparing to cross-examine a witness before a Senate investigating committee. Like the rest of America, the Irish community was split in its opinion of McCarthy. Many thought him reckless and irresponsible; many cheered him because of their strong, religiously-based hatred of communism. Above, Senator Mike Mansfield of Montana was born in New York City, the son of immigrant parents. Today he is majority leader of the United States Senate. Left, Michael Burke, once a secret agent in Nazi-held France and president and part owner of the New York Yankees Baseball Club. Burke spent many of his childhood years in Ireland.

surance to tax reform. Though Meany has had differences with black leaders, he still stirred the AFL-CIO into a front-rank role in the struggle for civil rights in the 1960s.

Before most Americans were aware of the issue of equal rights, George Meany, in his blunt, practical manner was part of the struggle. Told that black union members would not be allowed to register at a Houston hotel for a 1948 labor convention, Meany responded, "Either they get in or we get out." Everyone stayed.

While Meany presided over the "House of Labor" during much of the '50s, other Irish Americans were running the U. S. Department of Labor for Republican President Dwight Eisenhower. Martin Durkin, from the plumbers' union like Meany, was appointed secretary of labor in 1952. After some months in office, he resigned and President Eisenhower appointed another Irish American, James Mitchell. This Republican attention to Irishmen was a case of shrewd vote counting. In the 1952 election Eisenhower, running against Democratic Governor Adlai Stevenson of Illinois, had run appreciably better among Irish-American voters than any recent Republican candidate. The Republican party naturally wanted to encourage traditionally Democratic Irish voters to join Republican ranks.

At the 1956 Democratic convention supporters of John F. Kennedy's campaign for the vice-presidency made much of this shift. The urban Catholic vote, they pointed out, much of it Irish, had been crucial in the election of Democratic presidents Roosevelt and Truman. Put an Irish Catholic on the Democratic ticket, Kennedy men argued, and the urban Catholic vote would stop slipping to the Republicans.

Kennedy was not the Democratic nominee for vice-president in 1956. This convention campaign however, was the earliest stage of his 1960 presidential campaign.

Above, Joseph P. Kennedy (l.) father of the first Irish-Catholic president, and with him, former governor Alfred Smith, the first Irish-Catholic to try for the job. Below, George Meany, president of the American Federation of Labor–Congress of Industrial Organizations (AFL-CIO), has been working for the workingman ever since he was twenty-eight years old.

Al Smith had revealed himself by his clothes, his mannerisms, and his accent as a man from the immigrant sidewalks of New York. John F. Kennedy, by all appearances, was quite a different man. His clothes, his mannerisms, and his accent stamped him as an American aristocrat. Wealthy and comfortable from birth, educated at the best schools, Kennedy might be expected to be not the least bit Irish.

But there were other influences at work on young Kennedy. Irish America was never far away. His maternal grandfather, John "Honey-Fitz" Fitzgerald, mayor of Boston, took five-year-old John Kennedy along on his political rounds. Years later Kennedy would remember how his "old pol" grandfather confidently pulled off what has been called "the Irish switch" — talking with one voter, shaking hands with a second, and looking fondly at still a third. On more than one occasion, the Kennedys were refused admission to an exclusive beach or country club, and in this small gesture, they were reminded of the No Irish Need Apply signs.

Experiences like these, and also his books, for he had an Irish schoolmaster's love for books, put Kennedy in touch with his Irish-American heritage.

And so it was a new kind of Irish American who ran for president in 1960. John Kennedy was at ease in the company of the Yankees, the Irish, and the immigrants who followed them; at ease with rich and poor, black and white, Protestant, Catholic, and Jew. He was an Irishman at ease in America.

For Irish Americans, the Kennedy years were years of confidence. To be sure, not all Irish had voted for him. But even the growing number of Republican Irish were proud that one of their own was at last in the White House.

Kennedy's historic visit to Ireland was a joyous moment for the

Mr. and Mrs. Joseph P. Kennedy and family pictured above in 1934. From left to right, Edward, Jean, Robert, Patricia, Eunice, Kathleen, Rosemary, and John. The oldest son, Joseph, Jr., was absent. Below, the Kennedy Brothers in 1960 — President John Fitzgerald Kennedy; attorney-general and later senator Robert Kennedy; and Massachusetts senator Edward "Ted" Kennedy.

American Irish. In the Old Country he saw his ancestors' homes and prayed at their gravesites and he addressed the freely elected Parliament of Ireland. There he charmed and stirred his political "cousins" by quoting the Fenian John Boyle O'Reilly and relating the history of Meagher's Irish Brigade.

In New Ross, County Wexford, from whence Patrick Kennedy sailed to America, President John Kennedy's face gleamed and his foot tapped as children before him danced a series of traditional reels. Then a children's chorus began to sing about the rising of '98 and the boys of Wexford. Before long, John Fitzgerald Kennedy was also singing ancient words about a hero named John Kelly.

Glory-o, glory-o to those brave men who died
For the cause of long down-trodden man
Glory-o, to Mount Leinster's own darling and pride,
Dauntless Kelly the boy from Killane.

Within a few short months, J. F. K. was dead.

Daniel Patrick Moynihan — ever an Irishman in his gift for words — spoke for a grieving people, "I don't think there's any point in being Irish if you don't know that the world is going to break your heart eventually."

---❧---

TODAY'S IRISH

According to the Census Bureau there are 16 million Irish Americans in the United States. Who are these modern Irish Americans? Not so long ago they were easy to locate. Not so long ago they were insecure immigrants gathered protectively together in neighborhoods like Cork Hill in Boston or villages like Shieldsville in Minnesota. They married only "their own kind," socialized only among themselves, and worshiped their God in churches they sometimes had to guard

Above, an Irish dancing class for Irish-American children. Many families still maintain Old Country customs. The reels, jigs, and other steps as taught in this Bronx, New York class are drawn from a dancing tradition that goes back centuries to the pre-Christian era in Ireland. And (left) wherever the Irish gather, the presence of John F. Kennedy is close at hand. Even among those Irish who seldom agreed with any of Kennedy's policies, there is still a great, sentimental reverence.

Above, Irish-American Daniel Patrick Moynihan discusses political matters with President Richard Nixon. Moynihan, now ambassador to India, has served in the administrations of presidents Kennedy, Johnson, and Nixon. Left, Patrick J. Lucey, Governor of Wisconsin. Governor Lucey's grandfather was a famine immigrant from County Cork. After stopping long enough in New York to save some money, Grandfather Lucey (or "Losey" as he spelled it) moved on to Wisconsin where he worked, as he had in the Old Country, at farming.

against mobs. Now the children and grandchildren of those hungry immigrants roam freely and confidently across a land that is fully their own. The church doors have been thrown open. The old big-city neighborhoods have almost vanished and today one can find Irish Americans everywhere — in suburbia, in college towns, in retirement villages, everywhere.

Mostly the modern Irish are as secure and comfortable as the great-great-grandchildren of those "Yankees" who first came to America. According to the Census Bureau, most Irish-American families have middle-level incomes. Prosperity of this sort brings a contentment with things as they are and a suspicion of change. Thus the Irish, once fierce Democrats, began drifting toward the more conservative Republicans. Even the 1968 presidential campaigns of Robert Kennedy and Eugene McCarthy were viewed warily by these contented Irish because both men seemed too radical. And by 1972, a majority of Irish Americans voted with the majority of non-Irish Americans for Republican President Richard Nixon.

Today, they have settled into America and except for a fairly general tendency to celebrate every St. Patrick's Day, Irish Americans are largely indistinguishable from their fellow white Americans. And as they blend into the American landscape, as their transplanted roots stretch deeper and deeper into American soil, the memory of what it was to be Irish grows dimmer and soon flickers out.

Each day's newspaper brings a new story of terror and death in Northern Ireland. Despite the obvious distress of the oppressed Catholic minority in Northern Ireland, most Irish Americans are largely silent and unmoved. A cause that once served as a strong bond among Irish Americans throughout the country today exerts little or no tug. Irish-freedom fundraisers are sparsely attended. Rallies and picket lines attract the same few hardy, devout souls over and over. And all this at a time when rebel banners are again flying in Ireland.

The struggle for freedom and security in the Old Country is a distant battle, with little meaning for an American whose only bond is the fondly remembered brogue of a long-gone grandmother.

St. Patrick's Day. *From their first days in America, the Irish marked the Church Feastday of their ancient patron saint by an appropriate mix of religion and congeniality. First, mass in the morning and then, with the sun at its height, the grand parade. These pictures show some typical scenes across the country. In South Boston, Mass., two white horses pulling a wagonload of beer (above left) are helped by a group of burly men who pushed the rear of the wagon over the hill. Below, 1895: St. Patrick's Day parade at Fifty-Seventh Street in New York City. Above, St. Patrick's Day marchers passing St. Patrick's Cathedral, New York City. Note the Irish Republic's tricolored flag at right. Over, San Francisco Police Department Pipe Band in St. Patrick's Day parade (above), and St. Patrick's Day paraders in Detroit.*

Not all Irish Americans have settled down, however. Some, with fresher memories of Ireland and the hard immigrant days, cheer the progressive politics of a man like Senator Edward "Ted" Kennedy. Like Ted Kennedy and his fallen brothers John and Robert, these men and women acknowledge a heritage that includes centuries of oppression by a foreign invader, and decades of hunger and deprivation in a strange and often hostile land.

It is these vital Irish Americans who unfurl old banners and organize and march and vote so that life will be freer for their oppressed cousins in the Old Country. And it is these sons and daughters of peasants and exiles who remember what it was like to be poor in America, who work with and for those Americans — black, Chicano, Puerto Rican, and even Irish — who are still poor.

It is these living memories that the Irish gave and give to America — the memory of what it is to be an oppressed people longing for freedom, and the memory of a killing hunger. These memories kept alive by new generations of Irish Americans will work to keep America free and generous.

BIBLIOGRAPHY

Brooks, Thomas P. *Toil and Trouble*. New York: Dell Books, 1964.

Glazer, Nathan and Moynihan, Daniel Patrick. *Beyond the Melting Pot*. Cambridge: MIT and Harvard U. Press, 1963.

Greeley, Andrew. *That Most Distressful Nation*. New York: Quadrangle, 1972.

Handlin, Oscar. *A Pictorial History of Immigration*. New York: Crown Publishers, Inc., 1972.

Hoagland, Kathleen, ed. *1,000 Years of Irish Poetry*. New York: Devin Adair Co., 1947.

Jones, Paul. *The Irish Brigade*. Washington and New York: Robert B. Luce, Inc., 1969.

Kee, Robert. *The Green Flag*. New York: Delacorte Press, 1972.

Potter, George. *To the Golden Door*. Boston and Toronto: Little Brown & Co., 1960.

Shannon, William. *The American Irish*. New York: Macmillan Co., 1963.

Whalen, Richard J. *The Founding Father*. New York: New American Library, 1964.

INDEX

Numbers in italics indicate photographs.

AFL-CIO, 70, *72, 73*
All Star Game. *See* Sports.
American Federation of Labor (AFL), 39, 42
American Revolution, Irish in, 11
Ancient Order of Hibernians, 39

Bards, Irish, 42-45, 58-61
Barry, John, 11
Barry, Philip, 61
Beer, Thomas, 54
Berlin, Irving, 29
Bosses, Irish city, 35 36, *37,* 38
Breslin, Jimmy, *60,* 61
Brodie, Steve, *23*
Brown, Margaret (Molly) Tobin. *See* Unsinkable Molly Brown.
Burke, Joseph, 33
Burke, Michael, *71*

Cagney, James, *56*
Campbell, Timothy J., 35
Carolina Israelite, The, 62
Carroll family, 11
Carson, Kit, 25
Carthy of Blarney, Lord Cormac, 43
Catholic Emancipation Act, 10
Civil War, Irish in, 27-30, *31,* 32, 33
Cleburne, Patrick Ronayne, 33
Cleveland, Grover, 35
Cohalan, Daniel, 46, *47*
Cohan, George M., *56,* 57
Comisky, Charles, 51
Corbett, "Gentleman Jim," 51
Corcoran, Thomas, 64
Corrigan, Michael, 21

Coughlin, Father Charles, 63, 64, *65,* 66, 69
Creative arts, *60, 77. See also* Bards.
Cromwell, Oliver, 7
Curley, James Michael, 34, 36

Dempsey, Jack, 51
Depression years, 63
Derry, Bishop of, 8 (quoted)
De Valera, Eamon, *47*
Devoy, John, 46, *47,* 48, 58
Divers, "Irish Brigid," 33
Dorais, Gus, 52
Draft riots, 30, *32*
Dunne, Finley Peter, 38
Durkin, Martin, 73

Easter rebellion, 58
Education, 7, 18, 21
Elizabeth I, 7
Emerson, Ralph Waldo, 39
Emmet, Thomas, 8
England, relations with Ireland, 6-11

Family life, Irish, *55*
Famine in Ireland, 7-8, 10, 11, 13
Farley, James A., 63, 64, 66
Farrell, Eileen, *60*
Farrell, James T., 58, 59
Farrell, Michael and Catherine Kennedy, *60*
Fenians, 45, 46, *47,* 48, 64, 76
Fitzgerald, F. Scott, 58
Fitzgerald, John "Honey-Fitz," 34, 74
Fitzpatrick, Thomas, 25, *26,* 27-29
Flaherty, Joe, 61

Flynn, Edward J., 66
Ford, John. *See* O'Fenney, Sean.
Frost, Robert, 5

Gaelic tongue, 7
Gibbons, James Cardinal, 18, *19*, 21, 39
Goff, John, *47*
Golden, Harry, 62
Gompers, Samuel, 39

Hamill, Pete, 61
Harrigan, Edward, 43
Harrigan, Ned *44*, 57
Hart, Tony, 43, *44*
Hell's Kitchen, 22
Herbert, Michael, 33
Housing, 13
Hughes, John, 18, *19*, 30, 66

Immigrants, 5, 11, *12*, 13, *14*, *15*, 16, 17, *32*
Immigration figures, 2, 13
Immigration laws, 2
Ireland, 6-11
Ireland, John, 18, *19*
Irish Brigade, 30, 33, 54, 76
Irish Federation, 42
Irish heritage, 6-11

Kavanagh, John, 33
Keane, John J., 18
Kelly, George, 61
Kelly, "Honest John," 36
Kelly, John, 76
Kelly, Michael, 51
Kennedy, Brigid, 16
Kennedy family, *75*
Kennedy, John F., *4*, 5, 33, 34, 62, 67, 69, 73, 74, 76, *77*, 83
Kennedy, Joseph P., 66, 67, *72*
Kennedy, Patrick, 5, 13, 24
Kennedy, Robert, 79, 83
Kennedy, Ted, 83
Kerr, Jean, 59, *60*

Kilrain, Jake, 48, *49*
Knights of Labor, 39, *41*
Know-Nothing party, 16, 66
Korean War, Irish in, 69

"Lace curtain" Irish, 54
Landon, Alfred, 66
Lawrence, Abraham, *36*
League of Nations, 48
Lehman, Herbert, *68*
Lemke, William, *65*, 66
Lincoln, Abraham, 27, 30
Literature, 58-61
Lodge, Henry Cabot, 69
Lucey, Patrick J., *78*

MacNeven, William, 8
McCarthy, Eugene, 79
McCarthy, Joe, 52
McCarthy, Joseph R., 69, 70, *71*
McCloskey, John, *20*
McCormack, John, 64
McGillicuddy, Cornelius, *50*, 51, 52
McGraw, John, 52
McGuire, Peter J., 39, *41*, 42
McHale, Tom, 61
McKenna, James, 39
McLaglen, Victor, *60*, 61
McQuaid, Bernard, 21
Mack, Connie. *See* McGillicuddy, Cornelius.
Mackay, John, 27, 28
Mansfield, Mike, 71
Marshall, George, 70
Meagher, Thomas F., *31*, 33, 76
Meany, George, 70, *72*, 73
Mitchell, James, 73
Molly Maguires, 39
Moynihan, Daniel Patrick, 76, *78*
Murphy, Charles, *36*
Murphy, Frank, 64, *68*

Neighborhoods, Irish, 22, 24
Nixon, Richard, *78*, 79

Norman French, 7
Northern Ireland, 1, 82

O'Brien, James, *36*
O'Brien, John Paul Jones, 27
Occupations, 11, 16, 38, 39, *41*, 41, 42, 54-58. *See also* Politics.
O'Connell, Daniel, 8, *9*, 10, 29, 33
O'Connell, Denis, 21
O'Conner, Charles, 36
O'Connor, Flannery, 61
Ode (O'Shaughnessy), 6
O'Feeney, Sean, 59, *60*, 61
O'Flaherty, Liam, 59
O'Hara, John, 58
O'Mahoney, Joseph, 64
O'Neill, Eugene, 59, *60*
O'Reilly, John Boyle, 17 (quoted), 43, 45 (quoted), 76
O'Shaughnessy, Arthur, 6 (quoted)

Papal Brigade, 33
Patrick, Saint, 6
Politics, 16, 24, 25, 27, 34-38, 62-76
Population, Irish in America, 1, 2, 13, 76, 79, 83
Potato famine, 10-11
Power, Tyrone, *44*
Powers, J. F., 61
Powderly, Terence Vincent, 39
Prejudice, 11-17, 27, 48, 54. *See also* Politics.

Rebellions in Ireland, 8
Religion, 1, 6-8, 13, 16, 17-21
Ribbonmen, 8
Riis, Jacob, *14*
Riley, Bennet, 27
Rising of '98, 17
Rockne, Knute, 52
Rooney, Pat, 56
Roosevelt, Franklin D., 1, 63, 64, *65*, 66, 67, 73
Rostron, A. H., *28*
Ryan, Paddy, 48

St. Patrick's Cathedral, *20*
St. Patrick's Day, *80, 81, 82*
Saloons, Irish, 22, *23*, 24
San Patricio Battalion, 27
Scannel, Tom, 48
Scots-Irish, 1
Scott, Sir Walter, 8 (quoted)
Scottish Protestants, 1
Secret societies in Ireland, 8
Shields, James, 25, *26*, 27
Slavery, 7, 29, 30
Smith, Al, 62, 63, *65, 68, 72*, 74
Social life, 22, 24
Spanish-American War, Irish in, 54
Spellman, Francis, 66, *68*
Sports, 48, *49, 50*, 51, 52
Stevenson, Adlai, 73
Strasser, Adolph, 39
Sullivan, Ed., *60*
Sullivan, John, 11
Sullivan, John L., 48, *49*, 51
Sullivan, Michael, 33

Tammany Hall, 35, *36*, 37, 62, *65*
Thayer, Ernest, 51
Theatre, *viii*, 43, 59, 61
Thoreau, Henry David, 39
Tone, Wolfe, 8, 10
Truman, Harry, 73
Tudor royal family, 7
Tumulty, Joseph P., *36*
Tunney, Gene, 51
Tweed, William Marcy (Boss), 35, *36*, 37

Unions, 38-42, 70
United Irishmen, 8
Unsinkable Molly Brown, *28*, 29

Walker, James, *65*
West, Irish in the, 25-29
Whiteboys, 8, *9*, 10
Wilson, Woodrow, *36*, 46, 48
World War I, 46, 48, *56*
World War II, 64, 67, 69, 70

ABOUT THE AUTHORS AND THE CONSULTING EDITOR

Timothy Driscoll, the son of Irish immigrants, was born and raised in Brooklyn, New York City. His travels to Ireland strengthened the ties he already felt to his rich heritage. Mr. Driscoll has been active in politics and presently teaches sociology, a subject in which he holds an M.A., at New York Community College.

Eugene Murphy is also the son of Irish immigrants and was also born and raised in Brooklyn, New York. He is an attorney and is the Executive Director of a housing rehabilitation program in Brooklyn. Always aware of his Irish past, Mr. Murphy has traveled in Ireland and plans to return there and gather material for another book. He lives in a Brooklyn brownstone with his wife, Margaret, a film editor, and their daughter, Jane.

William Loren Katz has long been interested in the roles of minority groups in American history. He taught United States history to high school students for fifteen years and has served as a consultant to state departments of education and to the Smithsonian Institution. Author of the award-winning *Eyewitness*: *The Negro in American History* (1967), Mr. Katz is now working on several books for Franklin Watts, Inc. He is currently a scholar-in-residence at Teachers College, Columbia University.